INSTITUTIONAL LEADERSHIP
IN THE CANADIAN FORCES

INSTITUTIONAL LEADERSHIP IN THE CANADIAN FORCES:

Contemporary Issues

Editor
Robert W. Walker

CANADIAN DEFENCE ACADEMY PRESS

Canadian Defence Academy Press
PO Box 17000 Stn Forces
Kingston, Ontario   K7K 7B4

Produced for the Canadian Defence Academy Press
by 17 Wing Winnipeg Publishing Office.
WPO30252

Cover Art Designed by: Accurate Strategic Marketing and Communications

Library and Archives Canada Cataloguing in Publication

Institutional leadership in the Canadian Forces : contemporary issues /
Robert W. Walker, editor.

Issued by: Canadian Defence Academy.
Includes bibliographical references and index.
ISBN 978-0-662-45199-0 (bound) -- ISBN 978-0-662-45200-3 (pbk.)
Cat. no.: D2-190/1-2007E (bound) -- Cat. no.: D2-190/2-2007E (pbk.)

1. Canada--Armed Forces.   2. Canada--Armed Forces--Management.
3. Canada--Armed Forces--Officers.   4. Command of troops.   5. Military art
and science--Canada. I. Walker, Robert William, 1943- II. Canadian Defence
Academy

UA600.I57 2007   355.30971   C2007-980066-1

Printed in Canada.

1 3 5 7 9 10 8 6 4 2

TABLE OF CONTENTS

TABLE OF CONTENTS

FOREWORD

The Canadian Forces (CF), after analyzing the evolution of its own post-Cold War leadership and professionalism through the 1990's, initiated the publication of a series of CF doctrinal manuals. These publications, released between 2003 and 2007, dealt with the profession of arms in Canada and CF leadership. The last two of the series were applied manuals that focused on the crucial aspects of leading military people and of leading an organization in which a profession is imbedded. The latter manual, *Leadership in the Canadian Forces: Leading the Institution*, identified the challenges to senior leaders, both officers and non-commissioned officers, and provided guidance to them, their staffs and others with a commitment to CF strategy and the CF's future.

It is my pleasure to introduce this publication, *Institutional Leadership in the Canadian Forces: Contemporary Issues*, the latest of our Canadian Defence Academy (CDA) Press releases. This offering supplements the series of CF doctrinal manuals, particularly with respect to the applied manual on leading the institution, by addressing closely related, current issues but also by expanding and discussing the issues beyond the foundational coverage on leading the institution. Such coverage is timely and necessary for a number of reasons.

The global security environment is complex, volatile, ambiguous and dangerous. Along with that global environment, the rapidly evolving technological innovation plus the changing nature of Canadian society and those of other nations dictate that Canada possess a strong and vibrant profession of arms and a robust defence institution. The CF therefore has embarked upon a dramatic and systematic transformation initiative to ensure that it is capable of carrying out its evolving national defence policy. This is an institution-wide transformation designed to move the CF still further from a Cold War military model to one with a fully integrated and unified approach to operations, strategy and security policy appropriate to Canadian and global needs. Such a challenging and ongoing CF transformation exacerbates the demand for excellence in all of our CF leaders, particularly our senior leaders responsible for strategic and institution leadership, and stewardship of the profession of arms.

The requirement for strong institutional leadership in the CF, therefore, has never been greater. That requirement necessitates substantial and continuous professional development of our CF leaders. The Canadian Defence Academy, among others, has responsibilities for this professional development of Canada's military leaders. The Canadian Forces Leadership Institute, as part of the Canadian Defence Academy and with its mandate for research, development, plus generation of timely publications, substantially supports such professional development responsibilities. This book, *Institutional Leadership in the Canadian Forces: Contemporary Issues*, will be of interest to those CF members, government representatives and others who are committed to their own professional development and who have or wish to have significant influence on the CF as a professional military institution. It is my wish that all such senior leaders read this publication, embrace the content most meaningful to them, integrate such knowledge with their own significant experiences, and apply the results to the maximum advantage of the CF.

Major-General Paul R. Hussey
Commander
Canadian Defence Academy

INTRODUCTION

Institutional leadership occurs predominantly at the strategic levels of CF headquarters and within the higher levels of the CF's various operational headquarters. As institutional leaders of the CF, and as stewards and custodians of the profession of arms in Canada, senior officers and senior non-commissioned officers (NCO), in consultation with engaged governing party representatives and public service executives, ensure that the CF fulfils its organizational and professional responsibilities. The requirement for strong institutional leadership in the CF has never been greater. The security environment is dangerous, ambiguous, and complex, demanding a strong and vibrant profession of arms and a robust defence institution.

As a result, the CF has embarked upon a dramatic and continuous transformation to ensure that the CF is capable of carrying out national defence policy. It is a transformation designed to move the CF still further from a Cold War military model to one with a fully integrated and unified approach to operations, strategy and security policy. It entails transforming the command structure, changing how the CF organizes itself, and enhancing the CF's ability to deploy on domestic and international missions.

Meeting these challenges requires CF institutional leaders who are capable of transforming the vision and the "commander's intent" of the Chief of Defence Staff, into concrete policies and actions that achieve the governmental and institutional objectives. To navigate this transformation through the restless waters of change, CF senior leaders are required to demonstrate sound and effective institutional leadership required for CF success.

This book, *Institutional Leadership in the Canadian Forces: Contemporary Issues*, supplements the applied manual *Leadership in the Canadian Forces: Leading the Institution*, published in 2007. The latter, "*Leading the Institution*", addresses the challenges and opportunities for senior leaders functioning at the institutional level of the Canadian Forces (CF). It is one in a closely linked series of recent CF doctrinal publications:

- *Duty With Honour: The Profession of Arms in Canada* (2003);
- *Leadership in the Canadian Forces: Conceptual Foundations* (2005);
- *Leadership in the Canadian Forces: Doctrine* (2005);
- *Leadership in the Canadian Forces: Leading People* (2007); and
- *Leadership in the Canadian Forces: Leading the Institution* (2007).

This publication, *Institutional Leadership in the Canadian Forces: Contemporary Issues*, will be of interest to those members of a professional military institution, and to those who seek to contribute to Canadian and Canadian military interests within the domestic and international security environments. It contains eight chapters organized into three themes, institutional effectiveness (Chapters 1-4), practical aspects in leading the institution (Chapters 5-6), and building institutional leadership (Chapters 7-8). The chapters, authored mainly by members of the Canadian Defence Academy's Canadian Forces Leadership Institute (CDA, CFLI), address current issues closely related to those subjects explored in the CF's doctrinal and applied manuals, most specifically *"Leading the Institution"*. However, this book's content expands and discusses the issues beyond the foundational coverage in those manuals.

This volume begins with Chapter One, "The Road to Transformation: Ascending from the Decade of Darkness" by Colonel Bernd Horn and Dr. Bill Bentley. It reviews the CF's historical background. It opines about the CF as a conservative and anti-intellectual institution comfortable since 1949 with the perspective that the Cold War was but a bullet away from becoming a hot war, and as an organization supporting large standing armies prepared to do battle with the Soviet militaries. For the Canadian navy, army and air force of that era, the mission was clear, the military knew best, and the military could work on its own. However, with this dependence on traditional military concepts, CF leaders were not prepared for the Cold War to end nor for the new world order to unfold, and then to unravel quickly, as it did. The mind-set of the Cold War no longer worked operationally, neither did the Cold War paradigm work for CF officers at the geopolitical and societal levels. During the 1990's, post-Cold War CF incidents of unprofessionalism occurred in Yugoslavia, Cambodia, Haiti, Somalia and Rwanda, as well as in Ottawa, eroding CF credibility. The Somalia Inquiry reflected the worst in CF leadership and set the stage for change. Post-Somalia, the CF commenced a slow and gradual 10-year climb back to respectability. Horn's and Bentley's chapter articulates the details of that climb and the on-going transformation toward professionalism and effective institutional leadership for the 21st century.

In Chapter Two, "Culture in the Canadian Forces: Issues and Challenges for Institutional Leaders", Karen Davis and Brian McKee present a range of issues related to culture within the context of the Department of National Defence (DND), the CF, the three service environments, and the climate of individual units in the CF. Beginning with a discussion of the relationship between leadership, unit climate and the culture of the CF, they describe the various dimensions of culture and the significant role that it plays in organizations, and in the military in particular. The chapter highlights the ways in which the greatest contributions of culture can result in both positive and negative outcomes for organizations. Within the context of social, political, economic and organizational change, for example, stability, inclusion and identity within the CF can result in undue resistance to change, social exclusion and disproportionate sub-group identity. Davis and McKee provide an overview of relevant research in the CF that has been instrumental in revealing some of the influential characteristics of CF culture, noting that there is much that we do not know about the dynamics of culture and how it interacts with institutional leaders and the continuous social, political, and economic change influencing the security environment. Regardless, institutional leaders are accountable for CF culture, the ways in which it contributes to CF effectiveness and CF outcomes, and ultimately the continued legitimacy of the CF as a self-regulating and professional national institution.

Dr. Bill Bentley generated Chapter Three, titled "The Canadian Defence Professional". As background, he incorporated parts of a regenerated CF Transformation, initiated in 2005 on the appointment of a new Chief of Defence Staff (CDS). That transformation initiative included six CDS Principles, the sixth being "an integrated Regular, Reserve and civilian CF." The purpose of this principle was to encourage a more integrated effort where CF structures were to be closely interconnected and interdependent, in order to ensure the best utilization of appropriate experiences and skills at every organizational level. Dr. Bentley explores this particular CDS principle, its implications and its challenges. He studied the close relationship in the Canadian military-civilian dichotomy, along with the variations in perspectives between civilians and the military at the policy-strategy interface. Bentley provides a history of the relationships, explores the character and context of the current situation, and identifies parallels and similarities, as well as highlights differences and contradictions. He then proposes a methodology and a model for realizing the concept of a "defence professional" built on a "sound conceptual basis... the concept of professionalism and professional ideology". *Duty with Honour: The Profession of Arms in Canada* articulated well the military profession with its unique Canadian structure and values. However, Bentley also describes in detail the bureaucratic professionalism of the Public Service Commission, its non-military, civilian, public service employees (PSE), and its public service goals, commitments and values. His exploration of the subject then is advanced beyond this generic PSE professionalism into the unique culture of PSE specifically in the National Defence department. Bentley's chapter provides a model for such "defence professionals", and explores their professional circumstances needed for success on behalf of DND when "working Ottawa".

For institutional leaders, functioning as a military strategist is a significant capability necessary for institutional effectiveness.

An effective military strategist integrates a deep understanding of the relationship between professional and organizational effectiveness with an equally significant understanding of external strategic cultures and the diverse roles of military professionals. Chapter Four of *Contemporary Issues* is titled "Canada's Way in War" and was authored by Dr. Bill Bentley. It addresses this country's way of war as, "in part, defined by the very nature of its civil-military relations and the tensions inherent in this aspect of national security", i.e., the interface between policy and strategy, and war and warfare. He goes further by presenting ideas for understanding a nation's way of war through the construct of strategic culture, dissecting its major factors, and discussing their relevance and application to Canada and its military. Dr. Bentley concludes with the question, "…what can be said… about 'Canada's Way in War'?" and then provides his succinct answers.

The first chapter in this book to deal with a couple of practical aspects of institutional leadership, is Chapter Five, "Institutional Leadership: Understanding the Command, Management and Leadership Nexus". Colonel Bernd Horn provides insights on the challenges of institutional leadership, and addresses current misconceptions of the concepts of command, management and leadership. He observes that, "Paradoxically, these terms are often seen as synonymous, or mutually exclusive." Such confusion about these aspects of command, leadership and management generates barriers to effective institutional leadership. Colonel Horn provides an analysis of the three concepts, emphasizing that differentiation of leadership from command and management is important to institutional leadership, and that leadership is the critical component for creating lasting, enduring change. Colonel Horn also emphasizes that another critical component necessary to support enduring change is a long-term commitment from CF members achieved through a sense of identity, belonging and professional meaningfulness. Understanding this nexus of command, management and leadership is crucial, as Colonel Horn explains, to establishing these dispositions in members requisite to ensure success with military outcomes at institutional levels.

"Institutional Leader Ethics", Chapter Six in *Contemporary Issues*, written by Dr. Daniel Lagacé-Roy, puts forward ethics as the very core of leadership. For institutional leaders, a significant role is to be, and to be seen to be, an exemplar of sound ethics. To be such an exemplar, an almost metaphysical comprehension of ethics, military ethos, professionalism, and professional ideology is paramount. To be an exemplar is to generate, and be seen to generate, good and observable practices, as such practices are perceived as appropriate behaviours that reflect strong ethics. Ethics "must be seen to be believed." Dr. Lagacé-Roy's chapter reviews the military ethos and the leader ethics of the 1990's, that Decade of Darkness. He reviews the more recent research on ethics, the CF actions taken to create a Defence Ethics program, and the significance of *Duty with Honour: The Profession of Arms in Canada* (2003). He also reviews a theory of personal identity development necessary for institutional leaders to understand the demands of ethical behaviour, a theory that can act as their foundation for an important shift from a manner of doing to a manner of being. Finally, Dr. Lagacé-Roy reviews current and future ethical challenges for institutional leaders.

The remaining chapters in *Contemporary Issues* address the building of institutional leadership as it was addressed in *Leading the Institution*. These two chapters deal with the foundational construction of a Professional Development Framework and its application to institutional leadership, and the implementation of effective learning strategies to develop institutional leaders. Chapter Seven, written by Dr. Robert W. Walker and titled "Configuring a Professional Development Framework to address Canadian Forces Leadership Challenges", expands upon the background research and foundations for the essentials of institutional leader effectiveness, i.e., the requisite leader expertise, the cognitive, social and change capacities, and a professional ideology. This chapter also identifies the initiatives that supported the configuration of a Professional Development Framework (PDF) template that supports a process of professional development across the continuum of leader levels. Steps described in the chapter include an enumeration of CF leader responsibilities, an articulation of organizational effectiveness, generation of a context-specific model of CF Effectiveness, exploration of leader issues, identification of leader metacompetencies and leader attributes, and integration of these leader domains with a continuum of leader levels. Appropriately, the relevance of the PDF is exemplified through six real-world and current CF applications described in the chapter.

The particular content of the final chapter, Chapter Eight, addresses the responsibilities of institutional leaders to ensure effective succession of institutional leadership through effective and efficient professional development of ascending military leaders. Navy Captain Jennifer Bennett authored this chapter after her substantial investigation of learning strategies and their effectiveness in diverse situations and with various learning groups. Her focus, predominantly, is on top-level CF leaders. Her work, "Effective Professional Development Strategies for Institutional Leaders" sought out the best methods of learning across the pedagogy-andragogy (naïve child to experienced adult) learning continuum. She identified the most relevant subject matter pertinent to institutional leaders in place but, more importantly, to those institutional leaders in waiting. Bennett's thorough coverage challenges current military leadership development and proposes substantial changes in order to generate greater leader effectiveness from leader development practices, recognition of the non-pedagogical (i.e., mature, experienced, intelligent and engaged, "non-child", adult, student) status of experienced military leaders. She recommends a redesign of learning strategies and methodologies away from standard pedagogical lecturer-centred means using subject matter experts with rank or authority speaking to a classroom of relatively passive, experienced, and mature listeners, and toward andragogical methodologies that can deal with significant challenges such as dynamic and experienced adult learners with accomplished and diverse backgrounds, generate the inculcation of professional ideology values, develop and enhance critical, conceptual, creative cognitive capacities, incorporate the capabilities of substantial flexibility in leader styles and processes, and comprehend and master the very challenging process of specific and sequential initiatives to successfully lead change.

The overall purpose, then, for *Institutional Leadership in the Canadian Forces: Contemporary Issues*, is to expand upon subjects of particular interest to senior leaders that were addressed in the collection of CF leadership manuals, particularly *Leadership in the Canadian Forces: Leading the Institution*. This book, *Contemporary Issues*, provides readers with more extensive explanations and more detailed information than that in the applied manuals. A select bibliography is included as part of each chapter for readers seeking still more enlightenment.

Only through a sound comprehension of the complexities of institutional leadership, integrated with a solid adherence to CF professional ideology, will current and future CF leaders succeed. This book of contemporary issues in institutional leadership is but one additional tool provided to assist senior leaders to meet the profound challenges around them.

CHAPTER 1

THE ROAD TO TRANSFORMATION: ASCENDING FROM THE DECADE OF DARKNESS

Colonel Bernd Horn and Dr. Bill Bentley

Nobody likes mistakes. Fewer yet like to revisit errors – to analyze, discuss or study them. They are often an embarrassment and remind us of our fallibility and shortcomings. It is always much easier to celebrate our achievements and success. That leaves everyone with a warm feeling. However, although it is always preferable to avoid making mistakes, once they occur they are important and must be recognized as such. They speak to our weaknesses as both individuals and institutions. They are signals, if not alarms, to warn us of deficiencies that must be addressed. In fact, it has often been said for good reason that one can learn more from one's mistakes than from one's successes.

Militaries have always been bad at accepting this premise. Mistakes are often construed as a sign of weakness or inability and many perceive them as potential career ending events. Such a zero tolerance of mistakes breeds an environment of risk aversion, micro-management and stagnation. It kills initiative and experimentation. And, it avoids examining mistakes in detail – lest blame insidiously spread its evil tentacles and taint others in the chain of command. However, this state of affairs leads to atrophy within an organization.

It takes strong will and determination to break from such a cycle. Normally, crisis is the only catalyst that compels leadership within an organization to take action, and even then it is difficult. The Department of National Defence (DND) and the Canadian Forces (CF), particularly the officer corps, found themselves in such a situation. By 1997, they had imploded and found themselves at the lowest ebb of their history. They had lost the confidence and trust of the government and Canadian people they served. They were stripped of their ability to investigate themselves. Furthermore, they were not trusted to implement the recommended changes forced upon them by the government and an external committee was established as a watchdog. Whether the leadership wanted to admit it or not, and they vehemently tried to deny it at the time, there existed some substantial and deep rooted problems with DND, the CF and the Canadian officer corps. They were caught in a decade of darkness.

The road to this sad state was a long one. The assault on the CF and its senior leadership in the late 1980s and into the 1990s was cataclysmic. The safe, templated and well-known Cold War paradigm disappeared almost overnight. The new security environment marked by complexity, ambiguity, an ever-present media, and nefarious enemies and threats embedded in the context of failed and failing states, overloaded a traditional, conservative and intellectually inflexible officer corps that saw the world in terms of absolutes. As if this was not enough, a government perched on a veritable crumbling fiscal precipice looked to the military and a perceived "peace dividend" to solve part of its problem.

Not surprisingly, these pressures stressed the CF. Scandals and the bungled attempts at dealing with them led to the loss of government trust. This was monumental. Equally so, however, was the effect on Canadian society. As the military's failures, notably incidents of wrongdoing overseas, as well as reports of opulent and/or unethical spending and behaviour by senior leaders surfaced, Canadians quickly became incensed. Exacerbating this situation was a DND leadership that was not accustomed to criticism or scrutiny by the public. The clear and present Soviet threat and spectre of nuclear Armageddon had always been enough to distract and silence critics. So DND leaders did what they always did – ignore the noise long enough and it will go away. They refused to explain themselves or provide information. They ignored or stonewalled queries believing that the storm would simply blow over. If the winds were too strong, they could always take shelter behind the well-tested barrier of "national security" and the condescending, if not arrogant, attitude that civilians should just leave military business to the professionals.

However, catastrophically, similar to their inability to anticipate, adapt or change to the transformation in the security environment, sphere of military affairs and operations, the CF completely missed the dramatic and profound societal shift. As a result, they lost the confidence and trust of the very people they existed to serve – Canadian society. The CF had dropped into the abyss. They had lost the confidence of both the government and people of Canada.

So, what happened? Throughout its history, the Canadian armed forces, much like most militaries, has been a very conservative and anti-intellectual institution. Moreover, Canada, much like most western nations, did not believe in large standing armies. However, in the aftermath of the Second World War, when two distrustful and ideologically opposed superpowers emerged from that conflict, the world changed dramatically. Exacerbating the political and military competition between the former allies of convenience was technology. The war had sparked exponential advancements in warfare; jet engines, advanced aircraft carriers and submarines, rockets and atomic and nuclear weapons made the world that much smaller, and countries that much more vulnerable.

By 1949, the West had created the North Atlantic Treaty Organization (NATO) as a hedge against perceived Soviet intentions at westward expansion. Soon after the Soviets created the Warsaw Pact, dragooning its occupied territories into an alliance to protect them from their fear of Western aggression. And so, Europe became divided by an "iron curtain" and soon fell into a military stand-off, if not an arms race. This European-centric contest soon leaked into a global contest – with much of the world falling into one camp or another. Faced with the prospect of nuclear Armageddon if the major antagonists faced off directly, the superpower competition soon played itself out in proxy wars in Korea, Africa, and the Middle East.

Throughout, one thing was always certain, or at least one was led to believe it was - the Cold War was just a breath away from becoming a hot war, one laden with consequence if the superpowers turned to their nuclear arsenals. And so, from 1949, the world was seemingly on the brink of disaster. Securing the Western way of life for a grateful citizenry were large standing armies prepared to do battle with the Soviet hordes.

This state of affairs had a great impact on Canada and its armed forces. For the first time in its history, it maintained a large standing army. In fact, it deployed a large force overseas – including a heavy mechanized brigade group and a wing of fighter aircraft. This NATO commitment quickly became the *raison d'être* of the CF and all but consumed its entire focus. This despite the fact that Canadian Government policy always attempted to retain a robust second pillar for foreign and defence policy anchored in the UN. This created ongoing, albeit low grade tension in civil-military relations.

The Cold War, despite its possible consequences, was in retrospect a simple era for the military – if not its hay day. The threat seemed frighteningly real. Pictures of huge missiles pointed towards North America, impressive May Day parades in Moscow that revealed a large and very lethal military arsenal, the continued occupation of territory liberated from Germany in World War II and the brutal suppression of nationalist movements therein, reinforced the need for large Western forces. And in the event this was not enough, every year (coincidently around budget appropriation time) the US Department of Defense published its glossy *The Soviet Menace*, which showcased the Soviet Union's bulging military arsenal. In sum, governments and the public at large could easily recognize the threat. Accordingly, the military was provided with the necessary budget and was left alone to secure the Western way of life in the prosperous booming post-war era.

For the military, this was significant. They had a clear mission – counter the Soviet threat. And its implementation was left largely to the professionals. National security dictated secrecy and the Soviet's active espionage campaigns, which often were made quite public once compromised, reinforced the need for a heavy cloak of secrecy on all things military. As a result, the military could easily hide behind this veil to avoid explaining those things it would rather not discuss, and it did. Not surprisingly, at times, this list was quite large. However, the threat mitigated disclosure and the public was content not to interfere, trusting its politicians and military professionals were acting in the best interest of the state. Therefore, a very closed mindset, one that at best avoided public disclosure and at worst was almost totally contemptuous of it, developed. Quite simply, the military knew best – and those who did not serve could not possibly understand the context of national security. Therefore, the military was largely allowed to work on its own (within the context of its national institution and NATO framework) with little interaction with the outside world.

A second aspect of the simplicity of the Cold War was the operating security environment. The world was largely divided into two spheres (i.e. NATO / Warsaw Pact) and each was careful not to interfere dramatically in the other's. The actions and non-actions of such events as the Hungarian Revolution in 1956, the Cuban Missile Crisis in 1962, and the Czechoslovakian Revolution in 1968 (Prague Spring) provide clear examples of the unwritten understanding that existed. Supporting insurgents or proxy wars in theatres around the world (e.g. Vietnam, Middle East, Angola, Afghanistan) were always carefully managed. Rarely would the superpowers allow themselves to come into direct confrontation. Both camps understood and largely abided by the unwritten rules. Equally important, both camps propped up their surrogate, proxy and / or supported allies and ensured they maintained the global status quo. All together, this provided a great deal of stability during the Cold War.

Even peacekeeping during this period fell into the clearly understood model. Peacekeepers were only employed when both antagonists agreed to their presence. Their role was to monitor a ceasefire or peace agreement once the fighting had stopped. Their employment, therefore, was always within a prescribed boundary – in the buffer zone between the two former warring parties. Their operating environment was very clear. Each side had its fortified line. Each side was clearly delineated by its front line and all participants were in clearly identifiable national uniforms. Moreover, the entire operational area was quarantined. There were rarely civilians or press to deal with. When there was, it was under careful-ly controlled and escorted circumstances. Once again, the military was allowed to operate in almost complete isolation.

The relative simplicity of the operating security environment bled into the very fabric of the institution. The Cold War bred a very techno-centric culture. What became important was one's capability to be a proficient technical warfighter. After all, the enemy was almost perfectly symmetrical – almost a carbon copy of its antagonist. Inventories and tactics were designed to fight a conventional (and possibly nuclear) war against forces of a similar type. Everything was templated. Soldiers, non-commissioned officers (NCOs) and officers were taught Soviet order of battle and tactics. Exercises revolved around set initiators (e.g. the arrival of the combat reconnaissance patrol of a mechanized motor rifle division), which would indicate exactly what the enemy consisted of and where he was located. Based on the dis-tances from friendly front lines, it could now be determined what tactics he would adopt.

In essence, the key to training was learning the enemy's order of battle. As such, training institutions provided lessons, handbooks and exams on the Soviet enemy. Students would memorize the organizational composition (including num-bers of personnel, specific weapons and their ranges, vehicles and tactics) from section level to motor rifle division and higher depending on the respective rank level.

Furthermore, staff tables, NATO reports and returns and common doctrinal publications simplified operating procedures and tactics. NATO policy, dictated largely by the "Big Boys" of the organization relieved Canada of much of the burden of strategic, as well as operational, decision making. Canada's tactical role whether on the Central Front in Germany or its Allied Command Europe (ACE) AMF(L) [ACE Mobile Force (land)] role in Northern Norway reinforced the simplicity of the Cold War for the CF. It knew its role, its routes to the front, its actual fighting positions and the exact enemy it would face. As such, much of the training revolved around rehearsals for the possible showdown between NATO and the Warsaw Pact on the actual ground and exact fighting positions where this would happen.

Not surprisingly, this templated Cold War paradigm shaped how the CF evolved. Technical expertise and actual experience (particularly in Europe) within the conventional NATO warfighting framework became the key drivers for success. It nurtured a system that relied on the traditional military concept that leadership is a top-down hierarchical action that depends on unit command and staff appointments, specifically experience, as the mechanism to prepare individuals for higher command at the strategic level. Within this model, higher education was not deemed important. It stressed training (a predictable response to a predictable situation) to the virtual exclusion of education (a reasoned response to an unpredictable situation – i.e. critical thinking in the face of the unknown).

In fact, a rabid anti-intellectualism actually thrived. Those seeking higher education (i.e. a Masters Degree – as a PhD was simply unfathomable) were deemed suspect; individuals obviously trying to prepare themselves for a life outside the military. What was important within the military hierarchy were individuals who understood the system – the operating environment; the Soviet enemy; NATO doctrine and SOPs; and Canadian equipment, tactics, and staff work. Significantly, this fervent anti-intellectualism denuded the officer corps of individuals capable of, or willing to undertake, analysis, critical thinking, reflection and visioning in the larger geo-political and societal context. The inherent conservative and traditional military mind frame, compounded by its hierarchical, authoritative and closed structure fed a system that not only ignored, but actively closed itself to, outside thought and criticism.

In the end, the Cold War created a techno-centric, experience-based officer corps that was largely isolated from outside thought or criticism. Its intellectual development was severely limited and depended on simple experience and training, which focused on the application of NATO warfighting doctrine to prepare itself for World War III on the North European plain and adjunct theatres. Not surprisingly, its leadership doctrine was similarly dated. It revolved around a very industrial era model, which was output-related. In essence, if the mission was successful or the task was attained – ergo, the commander showed leadership (whether the task was completed in spite of the commander or not). If the task failed, the commander was obviously let down by his subordinates. Clearly, within such a model, mission success at any cost, became the key factor.

Throughout the Cold War, the system prospered for the most part. Commanders cloned themselves and thereby they assumed they ensured the well-being of the institution. Through the years, the myopic view and isolation created an officer corps that was intolerant of criticism, self-scrutiny or wider intellectual stimulation. Experienced Cold War technicians, who did not rock the boat and supported the status quo, tended to do well.

By 1987, the newly elected Conservative government and their bold new Defence White Paper, *Challenge and Commitment, A Defence Policy for Canada* was welcomed with open arms. It represented a reinforcement of the Cold War mentality – large conventional forces such as heavy mechanized forces in Germany and nuclear submarines. It also represented a halt to the continual downward spiral of defence spending that started in 1964, with the Liberal White Paper, and remained unabated ever since. However, the Conservative White Paper, much like their government, was fleeting. And, it did not bode well for the CF.

Military commanders and the CF in general continued on their course oblivious to the environment around them. And then, their world collapsed. The Fall of the Berlin Wall in December 1989, which is now universally accepted as the end of the Cold War, left the CF and its leaders at a loss. What now? The Cold War was over. We had won. Moreover, with the war over, everyone expected a peace dividend. And why not? With the Soviet threat eliminated – why maintain large military forces? Moreover, the Canadian government was facing a colossal deficit that was dragging down the national economy, devaluing the Canadian dollar and scaring off foreign investment. So, where to find extra money?

Not surprisingly, DND became a natural target. With the largest discretionary budget in the government, it was a no-brainer, particularly since the war was over. However, for the CF officer corps it was the beginning of the end. The new world order quickly began to unravel. Former proxies and surrogates, now left to their own devices without the necessary economic subsidies to survive, or the security infrastructure to hold together fragmented ethic and cultur-ally diverse populations, quickly spiraled into chaos. Failed and failing states mushroomed. In their wake, civil war, ethnic cleansing and genocide erupted on the global scene.

Appalled by the scenes of horror and inhumanity beamed into living rooms by the nightly news, publics soon pressured governments to act. As a result, the West as individual coun-tries, as well as a collective entity under UN auspices, soon dispatched military forces to bring order to the chaos. But, the attempts were awkward and ineffective. The world had changed but not everyone had taken notice. The new missions on which politicians and military commanders sent their troops were not of the Cold War model. Contrived manpower ceilings and equipment tables based on cost control and the desire not to present too warlike an image fell short of providing the troops and the resources they needed on the ground. Attempting humanitarian aid and / or peacekeeping operations in an environment where there was still an active war in progress and where none of the belligerents welcomed the interference of UN troops created frustration, risk, and inefficiencies on the ground for the soldiers. It also showcased the UN's ineffectiveness in the new world order. Unable to reach consensus, unwilling to provide mandates with the necessary level of force, and unable to provide the necessary command and control structure to react in a timely and effective manner, missions floundered.

From the CF perspective, troops were sent into harm's way without adequate resources, rules of engagement or coherent engagement policy. At the same time that the CF was deploying a record number of troops on an unprecedented number of operations, its budget was being substantially slashed. From 1989-2001, the CF deployed on approximately 67 missions compared to 25 missions during the period 1948-1989. Concurrently, between 1994 to 1999 alone, the CF was reduced from approximately 90,000 to 60,000 personnel, civilian staff was cut almost in half and the military budget was slashed by almost $2.7 billion, representing a 23 percent reduction.

Exacerbating the crisis in operational tempo and the stress this was placing on CF personnel, a series of incidents began to rock DND. Operations in the Former Yugoslavia, Cambodia, Haiti, Somalia and Rwanda had incidents of unprofessional and in some cases criminal behaviour. Questionable shootings, disciplinary infractions, particularly drunkenness, as well as black marketeering and the misappropriation of funds and resources created scandals. Concomitant with the troubles overseas were increasing revelations in Canada of questionable practices, particularly the use of government resources for personal purposes by senior officers in DND. Not surprisingly, the bombardment of negative press eroded the CF's credibility.

Notwithstanding the problems, it was the torture killing of a teenage detainee by Canadian soldiers in Somalia on 16 March 1993 that proved to be the catalyst that sparked the implosion of the CF officer corps. The killing was horrific enough. It tarnished the international image of the "do-gooder" Canadian peacekeeper. Moreover, it assailed the Canadian public's perception of its soldiers who seemingly no longer represented Canadian ideals or values. What made a bad situation worse, however, was DND's response to the crisis. Faced with increasing criticism from the media and the public at large, the senior DND leadership, both civilian and military, decided to stonewall its detractors. Falling back on their Cold War experience and mindset, they attempted to simply ignore the criticism and then when this failed they selectively released information often in a misleading manner. This quickly led to charges of a cover-up at the highest levels in National Defence Headquarters, which later were borne out to be accurate.

For the Canadian officer corps, it had reached a low point in its history. It was unable to foresee, adapt or even realize that the world no longer fit its archaic Cold War paradigm despite the substantial and significant geo-political and societal changes that occurred around them. It was unwilling, or perhaps unable, to realize this. Moreover, as is incumbent on all professions, it was also unwilling, or unable, to maintain its professionalism (i.e. responsibility – special duty to Canada; expertise, identity and vocational ethic). This last failing, specifically its inability to maintain a healthy military ethos (i.e. the values, beliefs and expectations that reflect core Canadian value and the imperatives of military professionalism) was catastrophic. Due to their failing, the Government and people of Canada no longer trusted them to regulate themselves.

An election in 1993 swept in a new Liberal government. Tiring of the public criticism and frustrated with the seeming lack of cooperation from DND, the government stripped the military of its ability to investigate itself and established the *Commission of Inquiry into the Deployment of Canadian Forces to Somalia* to examine the events and causes of the killing in Somalia. Not fully understood by many in the military, this action was seminal. It indicated that the government no longer trusted its military to investigate itself. As such, it stripped a key attribute of any profession from DND – self-regulation. Although many tried to deny the implication – the CF officer corps had reached a new low.

In turn, the Commission, frustrated by an apparently obdurate, if not at times dishonest, officer corps produced a scathing report. Of the 160 recommendations contained in the Somalia Commission Report, 112 were leadership and management related. In sum, the Somalia Commissioners found that "a failure of military values lies at the heart of the Somalia experience." Of the 160 recommendations contained in the Somalia Commission Report, 132 were accepted for implementation by the Minister of National Defence (MND). All told, he endorsed some 250 recommendations for change. These originated from his own *Report to the Prime Minister, the Somalia Commission, and recommendations from the Report of the Special Advisory Group on Military Justice and Military Police Investigative Services*; the *Report on the Quasi-Judicial Role of the Minister of National Defence*; and the *Report of the Special Commission on the Restructuring of the Reserves*. The accepted recommendations covered virtually all aspects of the functioning of DND.

However, the distrust of the military had sunk to such a low level that the government also established a "Minister's Monitoring Committee on Change in the Department of National Defence and the Canadian Forces" (MMC) to "monitor progress with respect to the implementation of change...." General Maurice Baril, a former Chief of the Defence Staff (CDS) conceded, "Undeniably, the 1990s represented the first strong test of the contemporary Canadian officer corps and we found part of it was broken." He added "experience in and of itself was not enough."

This realization should not have been a revelation. Thirty years earlier, another former CDS had already eluded to the danger. "It matters little whether the Forces have their present manpower strength and financial budget, or half of them, or double them," warned General Jean V. Allard, "without a properly educated, effectively trained, professional officer corps the Forces would in the future be doomed to, at the best mediocrity; at the worst, disaster." His warning went unheeded. But then, so did many others.

The very anti-intellectual and conservative military structure, in the absence of crisis, simply ignored the sage council. After all, the requirements for officer education, training, and professional development has been a long-standing concern. As early as 1947, Brooke Claxton, the MND, asserted that officer training was "… one of the most important matters to be dealt with in the organization of the Armed Forces." Indeed, officer professional development (OPD) has been the focus of a myriad of studies. In 1947, the Interservice Committee on Officer Training recommended that a university degree be the entry standard for any officer. In addition, it suggested that the Royal Military College of Canada (RMC) and Royal Roads Military College in Esquimalt be established as tri-service military colleges where aspiring officers would receive their university education. In 1952, a third service college, le Collège Militaire Royal (CMR) was opened at St Jean, Quebec to ensure Francophones had an equal opportunity.

Although the Canadian officer corps was highly credible and well-respected by its allies in the post-war era, OPD still came under criticism. Specifically, detractors were concerned that the system of officer development was unable to create a bilingual officer corps, and there seemed to be a large leakage of expensively-educated and well-trained officers who left the CF before normal retirement age. In addition, despite three service colleges and a subsidized Regular Officer Training Plan (ROTP), only a third of all serving officers actually possessed university degrees.

As a result, in 1969, an Officer Development Board (ODB) under Major-General Roger Rowley was created. Rowley determined that an OPD system had to satisfy three imperatives. First, all officers had to fully understand the philosophy and ethic of their profession, and be able to devote themselves spiritually and rationally to its services. Second, all officers had to master an effective level of expertise. Lastly, he believed all officers had to be given the opportunity to fully develop their intellectual potential. Concomitantly, he explained that the OPD framework had to be rooted in a clarity of mission and in a set of moral imperatives that ODB called the "Canons of the Military Ethic." These canons were Duty to Country, Duty to the Service, Duty to Other Members of the Profession, Duty to Subordinates, and Personal Responsibility.

The ODB also recognized the university degree as the foundation of professional expertise and reiterated that it had to be the academic threshold for entry into the officer corps. The Board also noted that OPD had to be provided through an integrated and holistic system of education and training that would take an officer from the pre-commissioning stage through to most senior rank levels. The critical component of the envisioned framework was the Canadian Defence Education Centre, where the intellectual and spiritual core of the officer corps would reside. It was from this institution that the concepts of military professionalism and officership, essential for the future effectiveness and well-being of the armed forces, would be developed.

Not surprisingly, the OPD system recommended by Rowley never came to fruition. Nonetheless, the ODB vision of the OPD requirement would remain valid and much of it would be resurrected in the Morton Report some 25 years later. In any case, subsequent to the ORB Report, there were numerous other studies, however, these were limited in scope.

The next major focus on professional development occurred in the 1980s and was focused on the requirement to address OPD for senior officers. The crux of the matter was the fact that the Canadian Forces Command and Staff College was the last formal training for the vast majority of senior officers. Although the National Defence College existed, its enrollment was limited to an annual military course load of twelve individuals. This was insufficient, particularly in light of the increasing complexity of national security issues and the strategic environment at NDHQ.

As a result, in 1985, Major-General C.G. Kitchen was assigned the responsibility of addressing the issue. Kitchen's analysis emphasized the social-political dynamic, which he believed the military profession, as part of society, had to be capable of participating in. Therefore, he believed this required the CF to furnish its officers with more and better opportunities for university studies, especially at the graduate level. The Kitchen Report recommended that senior officers pursue graduate education in civilian universities. This idea, however, was quickly torpedoed by another study conducted by Colonel David Lightburn, who deemed the concept impractical. *The Lightburn Study*, tabled in 1986, argued that the answer to senior officer OPD lay within a more structured yet flexible framework centered on national security studies rather than simply tinkering and adapting the existing system and creating new institutions and programs.

Ongoing concerns in regards to the shortfalls of senior officer OPD fueled additional work on the subject. In 1988, Lieutenant-General Richard Évraire tabled a paper on general and senior OPD that made three important recommendations. First, he noted that special course applicable to each environment should be developed for senior commanders. Second, job-related short courses and seminars should be created. Finally, he argued for the establishment of a centre for national security studies. In addition, Évraire also emphasized the necessity of CF personnel policies that directly supported officer education and training.

None of the initiatives gained much traction. In fact, with the end of the Cold War and the severe budgetary cutbacks of the 1990s, OPD took a major hit. The National Defence College, the CF Staff School and two of the three military colleges (i.e. Royal Roads and CMR) were closed. In 1994, General Jean de Chastelain, the CDS, commissioned the Officer Development Review Board (ODRB) under chairmanship of Lieutenant-General (retired) Robert Morton to "…review the education and professional development required by Canadian Forces Officers during their careers and recommend a programme which meets the requirements of a professional Officer Corps of the future." In all, Morton's committee made 280 implicit and explicit recommendations. They insisted that the weak officer professional development process in the CF was rooted in a defective and inadequate Officer General Specification (OGS). They also argued that there were major gaps in OPD philosophy, including "a need to develop a regime of professional development that has a military ethos woven into all aspects." The major failing of the OGS was to define all elements of the military profession, particularly the importance of the military ethos.

Furthermore, it did not define the specific training and education requirements for the four stages of officer development. In essence, the ODRB reiterated to a large degree the same conclusions and recommendations of the Rowley report 25 years earlier.

Throughout, education as a cornerstone of a OPD system was consistently stressed. The Morton Report stressed that the minimum education standard for officers was set at post-secondary school qualification, with the ultimate objective for all officers, except those commissioned from the ranks, being a university level baccalaureate degree. The Queen's Commission was to be recognized as the formal entry point into the profession of arms. Integral to the commission and throughout an officer's service was the requirement for "an exemplary understanding of the ethos of the CF, a commitment to duty …a high standard of leadership …and the specific knowledge base and critical thinking abilities demanded of a military officer."

The ODRB insisted that military ethos and ethics were core elements of OPD. They formed the framework within which officers accomplished their tasks. They also set the officer corps apart from civilian professions. As a result, each developmental period (DP) of an officer's career was designed to provide for these requirements. While DP 1 was the formative component of the system because of its critical role in shaping the professional character of newly joined officers, the remaining DPs were tailored to reinforce, mature and emphasize the leadership, ethos, and knowledge attributes of officership.

However, any OPD framework would be hollow if it did not have a sound, fully articulated military purpose. Morton recognized that the "primacy of warfighting" had to be incorporated into all aspects of the CF OPD system. Furthermore, the system also had to satisfy certain social and political imperatives. This included reflecting the bilingual nature of the nation Canada, as well as recognizing Canadian societal expectations such as the CF's role in peacekeeping. To implement the new OPD system, Morton insisted that "a statement that outlines a flexible but well-defined philosophy and system within which OPD can function effectively and evolve in a timely manner" must be created. He argued such a document was necessary in order to construct the framework within which coordinated and related policies could be developed. Morton also believed this would provide the authority and rationalization for resources needed to support OPD.

The Morton Report was not well received by the CF. Some reforms were implemented, including a review of the OGS to address some of its stated deficiencies, as well as to attempt to ensure that the document reflected the needs of the CF officer corps in the post-Cold War environment. An Officers' Professional Development Handbook was written embracing Morton's OPD model of four developmental pillars within four officer developmental stages. However, the ODRB Report's overall requirement for a total and comprehensive restructuring of the OPD system was ignored. The 282 "implicit and explicit recommendations" that the OPD working group identified in the report were determined to be "unmanageable." Instead, the ODRB Report was dissected and subsumed into the larger and increasingly strained CF staffing process. Those recommendations that were accepted still had to compete for scarce funds for realization. In the resource strapped environment, this was fatal. In the end, the ODRB recommendations had very little effect on the restructuring of the OPD system.

However, the crises in the 1990s, combined with the Canadian societal shift, which author Peter C. Newman described as a movement from deference to authority to one of defiance, forced the government and military to transform. No longer could either hide behind a veil of national security. The public demanded accountability, responsibility and transparency from its government and military. As a result, the message, which had been resisted for so long, finally sunk in. "The Army was forced to change," conceded Lieutenant-General Mike Jeffery, a former commander of the army, "I mean <u>forced</u>." He added, "The challenge is not to forget those institutional failures took place. We had significant failures." This message has not been lost. The tragedy in Somalia sparked a virtual reformation of the CF officer corps and the institution itself.

New appraisal systems and succession planning processes were undertaken, which importantly diluted the influence and power of unofficial "Regimental councils." Moreover, DND established a *Canadian Military Journal* to provide a forum for professional discourse, discussion and debate, and DND undertook a public affairs policy that was based on transparency and accuracy. It also put increasing emphasis on its obligations under the access to information legislation and undertook a multitude of change initiatives that addressed issues from employment equity, soldier and family quality of life, to more fiscally responsible management practices. Specifically, with regard to professional development a series of steps were taken, some concurrently, some sequentially, to address the problem. These stretched over eight years and indeed, some are still ongoing.

One significant early initiative was the establishment, in 1998, of the Royal Military College Board of Governor's Study Group, chaired by ex-CDS Ramsey Withers. This was significant because the Study Group was set up outside the normal chain of command of the CF Recruiting and Education System (CFRETS) and the Assistant Deputy Minister for Human Resources-Military ((ADM (HR-Mil)). The Withers' Report had direct access straight to the Minister of National Defence.

In the end, the eight-month study made two major recommendations (out of a total of 65). The first called for a new model for new-entry officer training, called the Enhanced Leadership Model (ELM). The second insisted that consideration should be given to the establishment of a CF University within the context of CFRETS. The first recommendation launched a seven-year process culminating in a modified ELM focused on the early military socialization of new officer entrants. The second required even greater pressure and took longer to overcome bureaucratic inertia and the remaining major barriers to its final realization.

In February 1999, the CDS appointed the first ever Special Advisor to the Office of the CDS for Professional Development (SA-PD). The first incumbent was Lieutenant-General Romeo Dallaire. The Office was created in part to demonstrate to the MMC that a concerted effort was being made to address leadership issues of direct concern to that committee's mandate. Even more so than the case of the Withers' Study Group, it was very important that the SA-PD operated outside the chain of command and reported directly to the CDS on a weekly basis.

Given the rank and reputation of the SA-PD this created considerable tension and even animosity between his Office, CFRETS, ADM (HR-Mil) and to some extent the VCDS. The lack of effective communication with the latter officer was indeed unfortunate since the then-VCDS oversaw the concurrent work being done to produce the important over-arching CF strategy document – *Defence Strategy 2020*. This strategy did provide a suitable framework for the SA's work and over time the VCDS began to see the merits of *Officership 2020*.

Over the course of a year the SA's Office developed the Statement of Requirement (SOR) for Officer Professional Development entitled *Officership in the 21st Century*. The SA's Office maintained a good relationship with the MMC and this Monitoring Committee was supportive of its work while at the same time tabling reports critical of the rest of the Department's response to the Minister's Report to the Prime Minister. In the MMC's opinion, at this stage, the CF was proposing tactical solutions to strategic problems. The MMC considered the focus of the SA's Office more appropriate.

Officership in the 21st Century was a compelling document that broke the log jam in the PD system and led to funda-mental change. In essence, the SOR recommended the disbandment of CFRETS and, in more detail than in the Withers' Report, described the requirement for a CF University. The SOR also strongly recommended the establishment of a CF Leadership Institute responsible for research and the creation and promulgation of doctrine and concept development in regards to leadership and the profession of arms. This Institute was created in 2001, very shortly after the publication of *Officership in the 21st Century*.

Armed Forces Council considered the SOR at the end of 1999. Although there was general support for several of its themes, there was great consternation that the document did not have sufficient "buy-in" throughout the Department. Ironically, this comment was made despite the fact that over the previous year numerous attempts at collaboration by the SA's staff had been either ignored or rebuffed.

Caught in something of a dilemma, with his own SA's advice being challenged by his senior staff, the CDS directed that the SOR go through another round of analysis with widespread participation throughout the CF. This was duly undertaken using the so-called "Empowerment Model." A series of large working group meetings, in three tiers – junior, intermediate and senior ranks – took place over the next six months. Ultimately, the revised SOR, now entitled *Officership 2020*, received formal endorsement by both the CDS and the Minister of National Defence.

This was a critical moment in the transformation agenda discussed in this article. With the support not only of the Minister, but also now by both the CDS and the VCDS, real progress could be made. *Officership 2020* set eight strategic objectives for the long-term professional development of the officer corps. Importantly, it also specified concrete initiatives to make such progress possible. Of particular note was yet another endorsement of the CF University concept to ensure that the education pillar of professional development would receive the much needed attention that it deserved.

Secondly, *Officership 2020* proposed the creation of three CF wide Capstone manuals – the profession of arms in Canada manual to define, describe and explain the concept of Canadian military professionalism; a leadership manual to update leadership doctrine last reviewed in the 1970s; and a CF strategic doctrine manual to provide the context for PD for the next 20 years.

While beginning the research to write these manuals, the SA's Office also turned its attention to the non-commissioned member (NCM) corps. If anything, Canadian NCMs were more mired in the conventional Cold War mind-set than the officer corps. In addition, if the officer corps was to be fundamentally reformed what needed to be done with NCMs? Four senior, experienced chief warrant officers were added to the SA's staff and an extensive analysis of the NCM Corps of 2020 was conducted. The result was *NCM Corps 2020* a strategic document that initiated a virtual paradigm shift in the concept of the NCM Corps and how it was to be developed. To be sure, there was, and still is, considerable resistance to the new construct that envisages a much higher educational component in NCM PD and new, more demanding, roles and responsibilities for NCMs. This in turn necessitates a different approach to the officer/NCM team. Nonetheless, considerable progress is being made.

In terms of structure, the major result of *NCM Corps 2020* was the establishment of the NCM PD Centre in St. Jean, Quebec. The Centre is now the focus for innovative thinking about NCM PD and the delivery of modern, challenging leadership courses from the rank of master-corporal to chief petty officer 1st Class/chief warrant officer.

While the SA's Office was working on *NCM Corps 2020*, the VCDS engaged the services of a private consulting firm to examine and make recommendations concerning the overall structure of common PD throughout the CF. Based on the work done in the Withers' Study, the Dallaire SOR and *Officership 2020*, they focused on the concept of a CF University. The original idea in the Withers' Study that such an organization could be created within the CFRETS framework had failed. CFRETS simply could not understand the vision. Consequently, the consulting firm's strong recommendation was to establish what was now referred to as the Canadian Defence Academy, with the Royal Military College of Canada (RMC) and the CF Leadership Institute (CFLI) acting as its academic engine.

The Canadian Defence Academy (CDA) was officially opened in 2001, while CFRETS was disbanded. The new Academy Headquarters consisted of CFLI, the Directorate of Professional Development (DPD) and the Directorate of Learning Management (DLM). The first was to be the conceptual/philosophic engine of the formation, the second to direct the delivery of PD products and the third to develop new techniques and processes to deliver education and enhance life-long learning throughout the CF. At that time, CDA encompassed RMC, the CF College in Toronto and Campus Fort St. Jean, including the Management School and the NCMPD Centre. When CDA stood up, the SA's Office was disbanded and some of the staff moved to CFLI. Work had already started on two of the Capstone Manuals directed in *Officership 2020* - the profession of arms manual and the leadership doctrine. This work would now be completed by CFLI.

By 2003, the first publication was ready. *Duty With Honour: The Profession of Arms in Canada* was a seminal work that addressed many of the underlying problems of the previous decade in terms of professionalism – philosophy, theory and concepts. It defined professionalism as comprising four attributes – responsibility, expertise, identity and professional ideology. The latter attribute represents a claim to a specialized, theory-based body of knowledge and contains the Canadian military ethos. As mentioned earlier, the Somalia Commission's Report had stated explicitly that a failure of military ethos lay at the heart of the crisis.

Duty With Honour was designed to deal directly with this conclusion. To be sure, the Department had set-up the Defence Ethics Program in response to the Commission's Report, which produced *The Statement of Defence Ethics* purporting to apply to both civilian members of the Department and uniformed members of the CF. However, this Statement fell far short of the requirements of a truly military ethos. At the same time, in a separate exercise, a small military working group attempted to articulate the Canadian military ethos, the result being a single page of aphorisms that did not take root.

Duty With Honour, however, developed the comprehensive Statement of Canadian Military Ethos which comprised Chapter 2 of the manual. The ethos comprises three components: Beliefs and Expectations of Military Service (unlimited liability, fighting spirit, teamwork and discipline); Fundamental Canadian Values; and, the four Core Military Values of Duty, Loyalty, Integrity and Courage. This ethos, together with the common concept of military professionalism espoused in the manual now serves as a unifying force promoting a CF identity within which nests the strong single service identities of the Navy, Army and Air Force. It now serves as the doctrinal base throughout the CF's PD System.

The next Capstone manual addressed was, in fact, a suite of manuals. First, the conceptual base was laid with *Leadership in the Canadian Forces: Conceptual Foundation*s. Next, two applied manuals were written – *Leadership in the Canadian Forces: Leading the Institution* and *Leadership in the Canadian Forces: Leading People. Conceptual Foundations* established a values-based leadership construct based on the military ethos contained in *Duty With Honour*. The construct identified a Primary Leadership Outcome and three Enabling Outcomes. These were Mission Success, Member Well-Being and Commitment, Internal Integration (e.g. morale, cohesion) and External Adaptability (i.e. accept, anticipate and lead change).

Based on this model *Leading the Institution* addressed system level issues such as stewarding the profession, visioning and change and being a military strategist in practical terms. It targeted senior officers and NCMs and was written with the experiences of the 1990s clearly in mind. *Leading People* is an applied manual concerned with direct leadership at all levels. It emphasizes the military ethos and ethical decision-making and provides practical guidance with regard to achieving mission success while keeping the three enabling outcomes in appropriate balance. This suite of manuals was published in 2005-2007.

The road to transformation did not terminate with the distribution of the first editions of the CF Capstone manuals. If anything, the terrorist attacks in New York on 11 September 2001, the publication of the Defence White Paper in 2005, Canada's combat role in Afghanistan, and the appointment in February 2005 of General Rick Hillier as the CDS, had demonstrated yet again the ubiquitous nature of change. Perhaps now, more than ever, there is a requirement for a highly educated <u>and</u> trained, experienced officer and NCM corps.

The new phase of CF transformation initiated by General Hillier in 2005 affects the strategic, operational and tactical levels of war and conflict. It will require a highly motivated, well-educated and skilled Force for its full realization. Starting down the road to transformation in the period 1997-2006 is just that – a good start. Only if the anti-intellectual, mechanistic and linear mind-set characteristic of the Cold War has been truly rooted out will the CF be able to prevail in the complex and deadly battlespace of the early 21st century. The Canadian Defence Academy has a pivotal role to play in the rest of the journey.

SELECT BIBLIOGRAPHY

Bentley, Bill, *Professional Ideology and the Profession of Arms in Canada.* Toronto: Canadian Institute of Strategic Studies, 2005.

Bercuson, David. *Significant Incident.* Toronto: McClelland & Stewart, 1996.

Canada. *Debrief the Leaders* (Officers). Ottawa: DND, 2001.

Canada. *Officership 2020.* Ottawa: DND, 2001.

Canada. *Minister's Monitoring Committee on Change in the Department of National Defence and the Canadian Forces. Final Report- 1999* (Ottawa: DND, 1999).

Canada. *Dishonoured Legacy. The Lessons of the Somalia Affair. Report of the Commission of Inquiry into the Deployment of Canadian Forces to Somalia,* Vols 1-5. Ottawa: DND, October 1995.

English, John A. *Lament for an Army. The Decline of Canadian Military Professionalism.* Toronto: Irwin Publishing, 1998.

Granatstein, Jack. W*ho Killed the Canadian Military?* Toronto: HarperFlamingoCanada, 2004.

Horn, Bernd, ed. *Canadian Way of War. Serving the National Interest.* Toronto: The Dundurn Group, 2006.

------- *Bastard Sons: An Examination of the Canadian Airborne Experience.* St. Catharines, ON: Vanwell, 2001.

------- ed., *Contemporary Issues in Officership: A Canadian Perspective.* Toronto: Canadian Institute of Strategic Studies, 2000.

Taylor, Scott and Brian Nolan, *Tarnished Brass.* Toronto: Lester Publishing Ltd., 1996.

Young, Doug (MND). *Report to the Prime Minister on the Leadership and Management of the Canadian Armed Forces.* Ottawa: DND, 1997.

CHAPTER TWO

CULTURE IN THE CANADIAN FORCES: ISSUES AND CHALLENGES FOR INSTITUTIONAL LEADERS

Karen D. Davis and Brian McKee

The culture of the Canadian Forces (CF) has undoubtedly changed over the last few decades due to both internal and external pressures. Indeed, as military sociologist, Franklin C. Pinch notes, the CF has become "more democratized, liberalized, civilianized, and individualized."[1] Throughout the 1990s, the CF went through various 'management renewal' initiatives, culminating with the Military Command, Control and Re-engineering Team (MCCRT) project designed to 're-engineer' the command, control and resource management structure in DND/CF. Concurrently, the CF faced continuous public scrutiny as a result of human resource issues such as CF personnel actions in Somalia,[2] the quality of life of CF personnel and their families, harassment, assault and career discrimination against women,[3] and the failure to address psychosomatic illness suffered by CF personnel who served in Bosnia in the early 1990s. Finally, 'doing more with less' became the mantra as efforts moved forward to reduce the size of the CF by several thousand members in the mid 1990s. As a result of such significant challenges, CF leadership came under intense criticism and demands, in some cases including legislated demand for change. Senior leadership needed to react.

By 1999, the CF promulgated institutional strategy, *Defence Strategy 2020*, to shape the future of the CF guided by five strategic imperatives: development and maintenance of coherent strategy, nurture pride in the institution, maximize strategic partnerships, maintain a relevant force structure, and improve resource stewardship. In addition, new doctrine that simultaneously reinforces the traditional military values of duty, loyalty, integrity and courage, and re-conceptualizes various aspects of leadership and the nature of the profession of arms in Canada, has recently been developed and disseminated throughout the CF.[4]

Continued efforts to transform and align the CF to meet changing social, political, economic, and security demands highlight the importance of organizational culture. Many DND documents as well as the management literature recognize the importance of organizational culture,[5] and CF leadership doctrine places the responsibility for shaping CF culture squarely in the hands of institutional leadership. However, culture is often overlooked in most change initiatives in the CF.[6] Beginning with an overview of the relationship between leadership, unit climate, and organizational culture, this chapter presents issues related to organizational culture with a particular emphasis on the challenges for institutional leaders.

CULTURE, CLIMATE AND LEADERSHIP

CF leadership doctrine makes a distinction between leading people and leading the institution. 'Leading people' involves developing individual, team, and unit capabilities to exercise tasks and missions, whereas 'leading the institution' is predominantly the domain of senior leaders who operate at a strategic level. These leaders are responsible for the development and maintenance of the requisite strategic and professional capabilities that will enable the success of the CF at tactical and operational levels of command.[7]

Importantly, CF doctrine explains that neither type of leadership is about the conventional ideas of the heroic individual leader or the isolated efforts of one leader, but "is about sharing responsibilities of leadership, vertically and horizontally within teams, units, formations, and the CF as a whole."[8] The second key principle of CF leadership is that it is values-based, meaning "leaders are to be guided in their decisions and actions by the institutional values that define CF effectiveness."[9] The five core institutional values are described as accomplishing the mission, contributing to and acting as part of a co-ordinated and cohesive team, developing and looking after CF members, anticipating and adapting to change, and exemplifying and upholding the ideals of conduct inherent in the military ethos.[10] These values map directly onto the CF institutional effectiveness model that is driven by mission success as the primary outcome, along with three essential contributing outcomes: internal integration, member well-being & commitment, and external adaptability. The military ethos, which includes military, Canadian civic, legal, and ethical values,[11] provides the glue that binds and integrates these four outcomes.

In conjunction with these recent transformations to the CF's understanding of leadership, new CF doctrine defines culture as:

> A shared and relatively stable pattern of behaviours, values, and assumptions that a group has learned over time as an effective means of maintaining internal social stability and adapting to its environment, and that are transmitted to new members as the correct way to perceive, think, and act in relation to these issues.[12]

This conception of culture is heavily influenced by the works of Edgar H. Schein, who places outcome related to culture firmly in the domain of leadership:

> Culture and leadership are two sides of the same coin in that leaders first create cultures when they create groups and organizations. Once cultures exist, they determine the criteria for leadership and thus determine who will or will not be a leader. But if cultures become dysfunctional, it is the unique function of leadership to perceive the functional and dysfunctional elements of the existing culture and to manage cultural evolution and change in such a way that the group can survive in a changing environment.[13]

These new concepts of leadership and culture represent a fundamental values shift in the CF that impacts, theoretically at least, individual beliefs, attitudes and behaviours. Not surprisingly, CF doctrine holds senior leaders, as leaders of the institution, fully responsible for shaping CF culture within the values-based model of institutional effectiveness. Organizational climate is not defined or explicitly addressed in CF doctrine; however, a comparison of the major leadership tasks for leading people and leading the institution, does imply that the establishment of effective climate within a unit or organization is a 'leading people' function.[14]

Doctrine provides the guidance for leadership and leadership responsibility in the CF. In addition, practical 'how to' documents, *Leadership in the Canadian Forces: Leading the Institution* and *Leadership in the Canadian Forces: Leading People*, have been developed to guide leaders.[15] *Leading the Institution* reinforces the relationship between stewardship of the profession and influence of institutional leadership on CF culture through the elaboration of cultural 'embedding mechanisms',[16] first identified in *Leadership in the Canadian Forces: Conceptual Foundations.*[17] However, the doctrine and 'how to' guidance do not provide leaders with a recipe for accessing feedback concerning the extent to which they are developing the conditions that will contribute to mission success. All of the outcome values – military ethos, internal integration, member well-being and commitment, and external adaptability – are significantly influenced by the culture and climate of CF units, and the culture of the CF.

The active role that senior leaders in the CF are expected to take in influencing and shaping CF culture, includes 'stewardship' of the profession to ensure shared responsibility for a strong military ethos. Consequently, it is important that CF leadership have an understanding of how culture is shaped and influenced, the relationship between institutional leaders and institutional cultures and sub-cultures, including the ways in which institutional leaders both consciously and subconsciously influence these cultures. When change is forced by circumstances as dramatic as those that impacted the CF in the 1990s, it is difficult to determine which aspects of change will endure, and alternatively, the extent to which some aspects of change may be a short term adjustment to unusual circumstances, and thus at risk of reversion to previous beliefs, attitudes and behaviours. For example, public scrutiny and internally and externally mandated changes in the 1990s resulted in several changes in the way that the CF addressed various issues: senior leadership expressed increased commitment to human rights and diversity; leader development strategies were developed to enhance the professionalism of the officer and non-commissioned officer corps; and policies were developed to strengthen the social contract between CF members and the organization. Undoubtedly, the institution has changed. However, long held dysfunctional beliefs can continue to impact culture if not successfully challenged.

The extent to which such changes in strategy and policy become fully embraced across the CF, and thus embedded as enduring aspects of institutional culture, is difficult to quantify. Culture is a complex whole that goes beyond what can be observed in the hallways of the corporate headquarters. It is more than the logo, the mission, or the chain of command, although these are all part of the culture and are visible cues of organizational culture. As Richard Hagberg and Julie Heifetz point out, "The culture of an organization operates at both a conscious and subconscious level".[18] Primarily because of this complexity, and as Schein points out,[19] the nature of culture is frequently oversimplified. Culture is often confused with 'climate' or is portrayed as synonymous with organizational structure. However, neither concept captures the full meaning of culture although both are impacted by it or in some ways contribute to it.

Michael Harrison and Arie Shirom describe 'Organizational climate' as "… members perceptions of organizational features such as decision-making, leadership, and norms about work."[20] The research on organizations from a 'climate' perspective is rooted in studies of experimentally created social climates, first published by Kurt Lewin and others in 1939.[21] Although it has evolved to include several measurement approaches, generally, climate research is characterized by self-report survey measurements of various dimensions of organizational environments based on the perceptions of members of the organization. Within the Lewin tradition, "The 'agents' of an organizational system, such as management [and leadership], are often assumed but seldom studied directly. They create the climate that others work in. The 'subjects' of that system, most often the employees, workers, or subordinates, are the primary objects of study."[22] Importantly, climate research is not primarily concerned with the process by which social environments are constructed, including the role and contribution of individual members in its construction. Instead, the predominant focus is on defining organizational conditions and individual reactions to those conditions or dimensions.

In the CF, for example, unit climate tools have facilitated greater understanding of the relationships between morale, task cohesion, social cohesion, confidence in leadership, experience of stress, and effective coping strategies.[23] The Human Dimensions of Operations (HDO) survey has been administered in various forms since 1996 to deployed army units in Bosnia, Kosovo, Haiti, Eritrea, and Afghanistan, and a Unit Morale Profile (UMP) has been developed to measure the human dimensions of military effectiveness, including 14 dimensions of 'unit climate'.[24]

Climate measures provide very valuable information for those leaders predominantly concerned with 'leading people' in CF units. However, it is important that institutional leaders have a solid understanding of culture, including the ways in which it is distinct from tactical measures of individual perceptions and behaviours. While in some cases, the work on culture and climate that developed throughout the 1980s and 1990s is virtually indistinguishable,[25] Daniel Denison characterizes the relationship between culture and climate as follows:

> On the surface, the distinction between organizational climate and organizational culture may appear to be quite clear: Climate refers to a situation and its link to thoughts, feelings, and behaviors of organizational members. Thus, it is temporal, subjective, and often subject to direct manipulation by people

with power and influence. Culture, in contrast, refers to an evolved context (within which a situation may be embedded). Thus it is rooted in history, collectively held, and sufficiently complex to resist many attempts at direct manipulation. The two perspectives have generated distinct theories, methods, and epistemologies as well as a distinct set of findings, failings, and future agendas.[26]

While the debates have raged in the academic literature around the relative merits of qualitative and quantitative approaches to the study of climate and culture, very little work has been done to integrate the theoretical approaches and assumptions to determine how culture and climate research can contribute to a greater understanding of the CF as an institution, as well as the relationships among the subcomponents of the organization. When all is said and done, it is important to understand the merit of both climate data and cultural understanding of the CF and CF units as each provide valuable information for CF leaders.

Daniel Denison identifies three key areas that are important to consider in understanding the distinction and relationship between culture and climate: the capacity of climate and culture perspectives to explain the evolution of social processes over time; the potential to compare across different contexts and settings in the organization, and the relationship of each perspective to the ideology of 'managerialism' which is most relevant to leadership in the military context. Culture research typically assumes that the concept of social construction is valuable for understanding social evolution on a case-by-case basis and understands that value systems are impacted by various stakeholders, power groups and subcultures. Climate research is useful for understanding the impact of social context, making comparisons across different contexts, and accepts that there is a distinction between the creators (managers/leaders) of social context and the followers that are affected by the context.[27]

Within the current context of the CF, it is important to understand social processes/social evolution to inform cultural change and transformation. It is equally important to understand similarities and differences across units and sub-cultures to inform integrated and lasting change across the CF. There is considerable potential for leveraging the outcome of both climate and culture research in the CF to increase overall understanding of the organization in regard to both social processes and distinctions across various settings and sub-cultures. Much of this understanding is embedded within understandings of organizational culture.

ORGANIZATIONAL CULTURE

Academic studies of the culture of organizations first appeared in the 1950s with book length ethnographies such as E. Jacques 1951 book, *The Changing Culture of a Factory*.[28] Cultural perspectives in organizational studies, employing both qualitative and quantitative measures, started taking shape in the early 1980s.[29] Based upon symbolic interaction and social construction theoretical perspectives, the organizational culture literature generally reflects the assumption that "the individual cannot be systematically separated from the environment and that the members of social systems are best regarded as being agents and subjects simultaneously."[30] The assumption underlying this is that members of a particular culture are influenced by, and have an influence upon culture. In this sense, institutional leaders are both influencers and managers of culture.

In some respects, it is easier to say what organizational culture is not, rather than seek to fully explain what it is. Organizational culture permeates the host institution and operates at many different levels, from the highly visible to the collective unconscious. Values and assumptions are internalized within culture and influence the way members perceive, think, act, make decisions, and behave both on a day-to-day basis and in response to stress and unusual circumstances. Culture is learned over time and is relatively stable. It is omnipresent in our day-to-day lives, not only within organizations, but within communities and nations as the "sum total of all the shared, taken-for-granted assumptions that a group has learned throughout its history".[31]

For the purpose of analysis, Edgar Schein identifies three levels of organizational culture: artifacts and creations; values; and basic underlying assumptions.[32] These levels of culture comprise a series of layers of analysis, as illustrated in Figure 1. In much the same way as an archeologist must dig through layers of sediment to uncover older finds, so too the institutional leader must dig deeper and deeper within the organization to understand core components of the culture and the relationships among them. Don Snider, following on from the work of Samuel Huntington in1957,[33] Morris Janowitz in 1960[34] and James Burk in 1999,[35] articulates four essential elements of military culture. These include ceremonial displays and etiquette; discipline; professional ethos; and cohesion and *esprit de corps*.[36] In these elements we can still recognize Schein's layers of culture such that ceremonial displays may relate to the most visible (artifacts) and *esprit de corps* and ethos to the least visible aspects (basic underlying assumptions) of organizational culture.

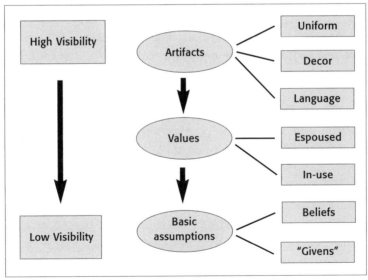

FIGURE 1. LAYERS OF ORGANIZATIONAL CULTURE

The most visible manifestations of organizational culture, the "artefacts and creations", include "… the constructed environment of the organization, its architecture, technology, office layout, manner of dress, visible or audible behaviour patterns and public documents such as charters, employee orientation, materials and stories".[37] Many of these elements identify the organizational structure that, as previously mentioned, can cause confusion between structure and culture. Identifying these attributes of the organizational culture involves, among other things, analysis of corporate documentation and organization charts, as well as observation of architectural features, employee dress, language and behaviour.

Much less obvious are the values of the organization, the next layer of culture. For Schein, the reference to values is intended to include only espoused values, 'what ought to be, as distinct from what is'.[38] Others have modified this concept to include 'actual' values, which are seen as having a more direct influence on steering or guiding behaviour.[39] These values offer rationalization and justification for action and although normally invisible to the actor involved, they can be identified and articulated. It could be argued that studies of organizational climate operate at this level of analysis and measure this component of culture. Through various approaches and measurements such as surveys and focus groups, as well as careful observation of interaction between employees, this layer of organizational culture can be fairly readily identified.

The most abstract layer of culture identified by Schein involves the 'basic underlying assumptions'. Values derived from actions taken in the past that have allowed the organization to persist become givens. They "... sink below the conscious level of culture and become taken-for-granted assumptions that organizational members use to guide their behaviours and attitudes."[40] Identification of these elements of the culture requires much more sophisticated and probing analyses of the organization. Prolonged observation of behaviour under diverse circumstances, detailed analyses of documentation, and in-depth interviews with key personnel and leaders, can begin to provide institutional leaders with access to this most fundamental component of organizational culture. It might further be argued that this cultural layer is the basis or foundation for all others. For this reason, it is frequently the hardest to identify let alone change. However, to understand institutional culture, it is important to decipher the combination of the visible organizational structures and processes; the organizational strategies, goals and philosophies; and the processes that connect strategy to the basic underlying assumptions that are shared by members of the culture.[41] As culture plays a powerful role within organizations, including the CF, commitment to understanding these processes is important.

ROLE OF ORGANIZATIONAL CULTURE

As networks of human relationships, cultures provide stability and a sense of belonging or identity for its members. In fact, it has been noted that, "As a stabilizing force in human systems, culture is one of the most difficult aspects to manage in a climate of perpetual change".[42] Stability represents comfort in times of change; however, stability or the human need for stability can present a significant barrier to effective change. The greater the alignment between the various cultural influences embodied within an organization, the less likely that dominant cultural norms will create conflict. The historical stability of a culture will be particularly comforting for those who are strongly aligned with the culture in terms of the roots of their individual identities.

At a very general level, organizational culture unifies the institution and distinguishes it and its members from others. It is the vehicle for the perpetuation of the organization and for the mitigation, synthesis and rationalization of change. The fact that culture is such an all-inclusive, multi-faceted concept means that it can serve many functions. All too often, this has led to studies that focus on only one or a few of these many functions and roles, excluding others from analysis.[43] Much of the focus of the literature on organizational culture emphasizes its role as a tool for inclusion. Attention is paid to the cohesive aspects of culture, "…as a defence against the unknown and a means of providing stability".[44] These elements of culture are valid and important. They provide parameters around the institution that allow people to operate effectively and comfortably within the system, socialize or regulate the absorption of new members, and maintain an identity over time. However, the other face of this aspect of culture, often ignored, is that it can function to exclude. The same processes and cultural elements may be brought to bear to include some and exclude others. Culture then is dynamic and situation dependent, allowing for opposing roles of unification and differentiation.

The range of ways in which the actors involved may use culture has given rise to numerous theoretical perspectives which focus on particular aspects of culture. Donald Bolon and Douglas Bolon list seven different approaches to culture captured in their comprehensive review of the literature. Among other things, culture has been viewed as an exchange-regulator, a control mechanism for handling complex exchange relations; as a 'social glue', again highlighting the inclusive nature of the concept, and as a scared cow, where values are idealized and remain untouchable.[45] The authors further specify analyses of culture that perceive it as 'a control device'; as 'disorder'; as a 'psychic prison'; and as world closure which '… prevents people from understanding social reality'.[46]

Clearly, culture can be examined from various perspectives and within different contexts. Understandings of culture vary depending on the situation, the period of study, the components under analysis, and perhaps most importantly, depending on the organization itself. The bottom line is that organizational culture can be a very powerful tool for leaders. Military organizations, including the CF, are extremely dependent on culture to fulfill many roles including the following:

- Define boundaries

- Convey sense of identity for its members

- Create commitment to something larger than individual self-interests

- Enhance stability

- Provide social glue that holds the organization together by providing appropriate standards for behaviour

- Act as a control mechanism to guide and shape peoples' attitudes and behaviours

- Help members make sense of the organization.[47]

However, it is also important to note, that culture can be powerful in ways that are not aligned with organizational strategy and effectiveness outcomes, including exclusion of valuable members and reinforcement of values, attitudes and behaviours that are dysfunctional in changing operational environments. The nature of military organizations exacerbates the strengths and weaknesses of organizational culture.

MILITARY ORGANIZATIONAL CULTURE

It has been argued that military organizations are unlike any other public or private institution. While sharing the same fundamental cultural influences as other organizations within a given community, nation, or theatre of operations, they frequently view themselves, and more importantly are viewed by many others, as unique. According to Joseph Soeters, Donna Winslow, and Alice Weibull, for example, "Uniformed organizations are peculiar. They represent specific occupational cultures that are relatively isolated from society".[48] The very nature of the mission for which militaries are intended, also sets them apart from other public or private institutions within the host society. As Snider puts it, "Military cultures derive from the purpose or tasks for which society raises militaries".[49] While it could also be said that all organizational cultures derive from their purpose, military institutions remain alone in their prime purpose. Warfighting, argues Snider, "... still determines the central beliefs, values and complex symbolic formations that define military culture".[50]

Given the changing nature of security, it can be argued that it might be more appropriate to describe the military mission

39

more broadly by defining warfighting as upholding or securing peace by the force of arms. This more encompassing definition of the core military function still has as its central focus the notion of the legally and politically sanctioned use of weapons. In this case, the use of arms is not only to wage war but also to defend or maintain peace either within or outside of the national boundaries. This unique mission has given rise to a unique organizational culture; one that Joe Sharpe and Allan English argue is different in Canada than elsewhere in the world.[51]

For Snider, discipline relates to, "The orderly conduct of military personnel whether individually or in formation in battle or in garrison and most often prescribed by their officers in command".[52] Recognizing trends and developments in the postwar period, he asserts that militaries now exercise discipline not through "authoritarian domination", as in the past, but by means of "manipulation, persuasion and group consensus".[53] Professional ethos describes the collective understanding of the values, attitudes and perspectives of military personnel. It includes the norms, code of conduct, and distinctive worldview of those sharing the profession of arms.[54] According to Colonel Mike Capstick, some of the important aspects of ethos, at least in the Canadian context are integrity, courage, loyalty and self-discipline.[55] These characteristics of the ethos are shaped not only by the military mission and the nature of conflict but also by external influences including international and national laws and codes of conduct, and the values and beliefs of the overarching national culture within which the military operates. The role of professional ethos and ideology within CF leadership doctrine is an essential aspect of self-regulation and discipline in the CF. The powerful and symbiotic relationship between ethos and culture highlights the importance of understanding cultural dynamics across strategic, operational and tactical levels. Ethos is a powerful tool for achieving mission success; however, military ethos can also take on distorted proportions, if legitimized and rationalized by cultural assumptions that do not reflect strategic intent.

One of the more obvious differences between military and other organizations is the greater use of ceremonial displays and etiquette in the former. Central to this overt show of difference are, among many other things, the artifacts, trophies, parades, and salutes that are the hallmarks of military life. Such displays are often designed to show the discipline and *esprit de corps* among members of the organization. Discipline and esprit de corps are seen as contributing to the cohesiveness of the group. It is this cohesiveness in battle that many view as vital to military success. For this reason, militaries spend much time in developing a strong collective sense to replace the sense of self. In combat, members of the team will be more likely to look after each other in spite of the risks, and to follow orders regardless of their own views on the effectiveness of the plan of action.

As with other organizational cultures, so too with the military, those cultural elements that are drawn on at any given time depend in part on the circumstances or situation faced by the actor involved. Certain military activities would be unacceptable in peacetime but perfectly legitimate in a war or crisis situation. Soeters *et al* introduce the concept of 'hot' and 'cold' conditions to denote times and circumstances of varying military activity and pace of operations. Routine garrison duty becomes a cold condition requiring low-intensity and generally safe activity, whereas highly volatile or active duties such as those onboard an aircraft carrier in a war zone would be considered hot.[56] Within larger organizations, situational differences such as these can, over time, lead to the development of subgroups within the larger whole developing what some refer to as 'sub-cultures'.

In the CF, in spite of such variations, frequently the focus is on the need to develop a CF-wide culture that will enable the efforts of individuals and teams at all levels in ensuring the integrity of the profession of arms, promoting the development of effective leaders, encouraging life-long learning, supporting innovation, understanding and promoting diversity, and providing the foundation for a strong officer/NCM leadership team.[57] The ideal CF culture is described as a learning organization facilitated by trust, ethical decision-making, social integration, horizontal networking, collegiality, empowered responsibility, and accountability balanced with intelligent risk-taking. In achieving this ideal, there are calls for CF culture to shift, for example, from a 'need to know' to a 'need to share' paradigm.[58]

However, the CF is comprised of three environmental service cultures – land, air and sea. Within each of these cultures there are numerous sub-cultures linked to regiments, squadrons, ships, occupations and occupation groups, and rank groups. Furthermore, to varying degrees, at various times, 'hot' and 'cold' conditions will impact unit climates, cultures and group member identity. These groups are also influenced by numerous shared social and historical understandings that find their roots in European-based military culture, customs and traditions. Individual identities within and across various sub-units and their associated cultures are further influenced by history, language, gender, ethnicity, socio-economic status, and experience. In the CF, unique sub-group identity is visible by environmental uniforms as well as uniform insignia identifying various ships, squadrons, and regiments.

Sub-group identity is important in reinforcing group morale and military ethos. On the other hand, excessive sub-group cultural identity can also serve to reinforce values, beliefs and responses, to new and changing circumstances in particular, that are not aligned with the values of the CF and Canadian society.[59] Visible sub-group identifiers represent the 'tip of the iceberg' in terms of the values, beliefs and practices within a particular unit. Undue focus on unit distinctions may also create false cultural boundaries in terms of where and how culture is manifested within and across various parts of the organization. That is, culture in the CF is not necessarily contained within CF-defined structure, however tempting it may be to simplify cultural impact by linking various cultural characteristics to specific sub-groups within the CF. It is important to understand this social construction of diversity within and among CF units, including a critical examination of the formation of underlying taken-for-granted assumptions, values and practices that are considered legitimate.[60] This is central to understanding the extent to which sub-cultures reflect the CF strategic values framework, including the development and sustainment of an appropriate relationship with the host society.

THE MILITARY AND SOCIETY

Gail Zellman *et al* neatly summarize the core elements of military culture as, "…conservative, rooted in history and tradition, based on group loyalty and conformity and oriented toward obedience to superiors."[61] Defined in this way, the potential gulf that may exist between military and civilian organizational culture is apparent. The emergence and increased domination of relatively new, non-traditional, 'flat' organizations espousing more egalitarian views stand in stark contrast to this, admittedly traditional definition, of military organizational culture. However, such articulations of the constituent elements of military culture may be said only to accentuate existing differences. For this reason, much thought has been given, particularly in the United States, to the acceptable gap between the military and civilian worlds.[62] Within the CF context, external adaptability is an essential value outcome informing the relationship between Canadian society and the CF.

Nowhere is the role of leading the institution more important than within the context and expectations of Canadian society. The values and priorities of an increasingly socially and demographically diverse society and the legal and political institutions sanctioned by that society have a significant impact on the role of the CF. Leadership in the DND and CF share a responsibility to Canadians to ensure that defence practices and processes are indeed the most effective and efficient means possible to meet societal and government expectations. As a minimum, the CF must comply with legislation and participate effectively with security environment partners in Canada. However, the minimum is not enough. Compliance with human rights legislation in Canada, for example, represents the minimum. Complying with legislation, as well as embracing the values of Canadian society through CF commitment to processes such as gender integration will ensure that the CF is perceived as credible and relevant within Canada. It is important that leaders of the institution participate fully in Canadian society and openly embrace the expectations of Canadians in terms of full transparency and social responsibility. In meeting these expectations, leaders of the institution provide an institutional voice – a cultural link – to Canadian society and actively engage in the business of national security with the government and the public.[63] Persistent initiatives to build inter-agency knowledge networks, and shared decision-making processes are dependent upon commitment to security for Canadians, through combined DND and CF effort.

The extent to which culture, external to the CF, impacts CF organizational culture(s) is also an important, but challenging, consideration for institutional leaders. In addition, 'culture' finds its origins, and is represented, in various forms outside of the boundaries of organizations. In this broader sense, culture can be understood as a collective noun for the symbolic and learned aspects of human society that include language, custom and convention representing a realm of beliefs, ideas, practices, and ways of living.[64] Culture and cultural identities within society are complex and multiple, and increasingly so as society becomes more diverse. Individuals may embody a cultural consciousness that is not simply dualistic (e.g. African-Canadian), but a 'poly consciousness' reflecting ethnicity, region or origin, language, religion and so on.[65] Increasingly, organizations will include multiple and complex cultural influences with varying relationships and implications for the organization. In fact, the inclusion of various cultural influences in the CF is integral to its identity as a Canadian institution as Canada becomes more diverse. This context, in addition to the increasingly complex relationships between ethnic, community, organizational and national cultures in both the domestic and international contexts, reinforces the importance of understanding culture, cultural processes, and cultural outcomes.

The character of federal government departmental and non-government organizational cultures will have a significant impact on both CF strategy and the successful implementation of that strategy in meeting the demands of the future security environment. These cultures are the medium through which institutional leadership will ensure the success of the institution. Similarly, an understanding of the public service cultural values, challenges and processes is critical to building multi-dimensional partnerships across government and other organizations. Importantly, building relationships outside of the CF is informed by institutional self-awareness; that is, knowledge of the strengths and weaknesses of CF culture.

CF CULTURE

Culture, as a key concept in understanding military organizations, started to gain momentum in the late 1990s and continues to grow rapidly.[66] Defence studies of aspects of military culture in Canada reach back to at least 1967 with a review of the relationship between sub-culture (English and French) influences and attitudes toward military service.[67] Several of the key investigations that provide important information about CF culture are discussed below. While each project reflects different methodological approaches and different theoretical perspectives, responding to different questions, they also contribute significantly to what we know about CF culture and/or sub-cultures.

The findings of the 1979 'Cotton Report', based upon survey data analysis, caught the attention of military leaders and served as a place marker for understanding contemporary army culture in the CF. The research presented in the Cotton Report was informed by significant changes occurring in the military at the time; specifically, the increasing number of non-combatant occupations, and general trends toward growing bureaucratic complexity, convergence of military and civilian skill structures, and the increasingly minority position of combat soldiers. Following on the work of American military sociologist, Charles Moskos, Cotton's research contrasted the 'occupational' model of the military organization with the traditional concept of the military as a unique institution with its own values, symbols and practices – the 'vocational' model. Survey data was collected from over 1,600 CF members in both support and combat trades, to measure numerous dimensions of values and attitudes toward military service, including military role obligation (using a military ethos scale); trade satisfaction and self-image; support for the regimental system; willingness to enter combat; commitment to the CF; leadership instability[68]; and identification with the army environment.[69]

Cotton's research was intended as "a beginning baseline study of the character of the Army in Canada,"[70] and his findings claimed to "provide support for the image of an army characterized by cleavages in basic values and assumptions about structure and process in military life."[71] In comparing attitudes toward military service across combat and support roles, and junior and senior non-commissioned soldiers and officers, Cotton's study revealed a significant gap between combat arms officers and junior combat arms soldiers; that is, a very small percentage of junior personnel in the combat arms supported the vocational ethos that was supported by their officers, and which their officers expected them to support. In addition, junior combat arms soldiers expressed dissatisfaction with the excessive turnover of leaders – over 65 percent reported that they had changed direct leaders four or more times in the past two years.[72] Although this research was not explicitly identified as a study of organizational culture, in the sense that it was a study of attitudes claiming to reveal basic values and assumptions, it did measure key components of organizational culture.

Donna Winslow's investigation, presented in the 1997 publication, *The Canadian Airborne Regiment in Somalia: A Socio-cultural Inquiry*, represents perhaps the most comprehensive study of the culture of a single CF unit ever conducted. Conducted from a social anthropological perspective, and based upon theories of identity formation, culture in this context is understood as the collective values found within a group or a society that continue to exist even after changes within the group dynamic occur. This cultural inquiry is informed by over 50 in-depth interviews with airborne soldiers, several focus groups with soldiers and some family members, visual records (e.g. photos, videotapes), personal records (e.g. letters written home by soldiers, first hand accounts written by Somali journalists), official documents (e.g. court martial proceedings), testimonies from the Commission of Inquiry into the Deployment of Canadian Forces to Somalia, and a review of studies on the deployment of United States (U. S.) military troops to Somalia.

The goal of Winslow's research was to explain how the culture of the regiment was formed and to what extent that culture affected the behaviour of Canadian soldiers in Somalia.[73] She concludes that several factors contributed to the events in Somalia, including tension between the combat and modern bureaucratic paradigms in the CF, unit identity and socialization processes, frequent rotation of officers contributing to a non-commissioned soldier sub-culture and authority system, and situational challenges in Somalia.[74] Winslow's research was exclusively qualitative and guided by the reasoning of inductive analysis and an exploratory research process to examine the various levels of culture,[75] including the visible organizational structures and processes, the espoused values, and the basic underlying 'taken-for-granted' assumptions that guide human behaviour.

Understanding Military Culture: A Canadian Perspective, by Canadian military historian, Allan English, is noteworthy as an isolated example of a cultural analysis of the CF as an institution. English asserts that previous concepts of military culture are based predominantly on the U.S. military experience and the related literature is largely rhetorical and focused on the traditional 'warrior' in military culture. He uses secondary sources to develop an analysis of Canadian military culture within the context of Canadian society, including an examination of the roots of Canadian military culture, the contributions of the air, land and sea sub-cultures, ethos, and professionalism. Observing that military culture is shaped by influences other than leadership, including civil-military relations, an argument is developed to support a multi-disciplinary organizational behaviour approach to the study of Canadian military culture. In conclusion, English warns against reliance on a single approach to understanding military culture, specifically the framework established by

Edgar Schein that many U.S. military studies have relied upon, as he believes it will limit understanding of Canadian military culture.[76]

A 2004 study of climate, culture and socio-cultural attitudes and values in the Canadian army, *Canada's Soldiers: Military Ethos and Canadian Values in the 21st Century*, includes measures of social and cultural values that compare soldier responses in 2004 to soldier responses in 1979, soldier responses across various army sub-groups, and soldier responses to civilian responses in 2004.[77] This investigation defines culture within the social psychological paradigm offered by Edgar Schein, and is thus parallel to CF doctrine in its definition – characterized by symbols, rituals, values and beliefs shared by members of an organization. Importantly, this research also notes that culture "determines how and why certain things are done in the organization."[78] Organizational climate, along with its relationship to culture is defined within this context as:

> ...how people feel about their organization. Satisfaction with leaders, pay, working conditions, and co-workers are all aspects of climate. Oftentimes, climate is influenced by the underlying values and beliefs that comprise culture. Similarly, changes to climate can result in changes to the culture over time.[79]

Climate is defined in relation to culture, just as the analysis presented in the 2005 army report integrates the findings of the climate and culture surveys. The climate survey component of this study builds upon previous measures used in the CF, including the 1979 Cotton research and CF climate research previously discussed, to measure a range of dimensions: individual attitudes and opinions in reference to the role of the army; mission accomplishment and troop safety; workload; ethics; institutional/occupational role orientation; careerism; professionalism; willingness to enter combat; discipline; confidence in skills and ability; leadership culture; perceptions of immediate leadership; right of association; learning organizational culture; acceptance of gender integration; acceptance of diversity; attitudes toward language requirements; communication; and locus of commitment.

The socio-cultural survey component of the army study measures individual attitudes and values on 67 trends determined to be of interest to the army including personal achievement and development, importance of the individual, adherence to institutional leadership, attraction to intensity, sense of duty and need for accomplishment, social conscience, and conservatism. Importantly, the responses of soldiers is compared to the responses of a sample of Canadians on the same survey items, thus providing information in regards to the differences and similarities between the military and civilian society. For example, the results of this investigation indicate that as a group, overall, the responses of junior non-commissioned members in the CF tend to highlight the strong emphasis that they place on being members of well-defined groups, and in turn, a potential tendency to exclude and even exhibit hostility towards others who don't share their particular membership characteristics.[80]

While this research clearly comprises components of measuring culture and measuring climate, the report of the integrated findings is identified as "an important first step in defining and describing the organizational military culture that exists in Canada's army today." Summarizing military culture as "how we do things around here,"[81] this research includes measures of army attitudes and opinions that are used to compare 'how it is' with 'how it should be' in relation to the espoused ethos in CF leadership doctrine, *Duty With Honour: The Profession of Arms in Canada*.

Finally, an ongoing CF research project design proposes an environment scan of culture in the CF, international comparisons, an historical study of organizational culture/and CF culture change, and a coordinated and consultative review of CF joint culture, army, navy and air force sub-cultures, reserve sub-culture, and corporate/institutional culture.[82] Early data collection includes in-depth interviews with executive level leaders in the Department of National Defence

(DND) and the CF, under the auspices of a 'senior decision-makers project' as well as a preliminary review of work that contributes to the current understanding of CF culture.[83] The overall goal of this project is to inform current understanding of culture in the CF, determine what aspects of CF culture need to change and how to satisfy the requirements of the future in a way that is coherent with ongoing CF transformation, and to determine an appropriate model for culture change. In essence, the project seeks to answer three basic, but incredibly complex, questions – where are we now, where do we need to go, and how do we get there?

The culture research reviewed in this discussion does not include the substantial body of information and literature that the DND/CF has accumulated under a range of labels, each potentially comprising an element of culture (and culture change), since approximately 1980. This internal research spans numerous themes including the integration of women into previously all-male units, incidence of harassment, ethical decision-making, quality of life, conditions of service, sexual orientation, gender integration, diversity, employment equity, mechanisms of voice, attrition, and retention. Studies such as these frequently make reference to the need for cultural change or the responsibility of leadership to take positive action and influence attitudes and behaviour.

In summary, what we know about culture in the CF reflects a variety of approaches to understanding culture. This review also reveals substantial gaps in available knowledge in relation to the dynamics of culture construction, existing sub-cultures, and the relationship between various influences on culture, including leadership and Canadian society.

DISCUSSION

This discussion builds upon the relationship between culture and institutional leaders discussed in both *Leadership in the Canadian Forces: Conceptual Foundations* and *Leadership in the Canadian Forces: Leading the Institution*. Clearly, institutional leaders have a profound impact on the culture of the CF through the policies they implement, the social norms they endorse, and the personal characteristics they display. In its creation, the culture of an organization is a reflection of the initial leadership and the societal culture within which it is located. Once established, the culture will define acceptable leadership within the organization for future generations.[84] Those who achieve career success and thus become the leaders of the institution, do it within the terms set by the organizational culture(s). Consequently, leaders of the institution who endeavour to change culture may find it necessary to change how they perceive, how they think, and how they lead if they expect to be successful in changing the cultural expectations for what constitutes effective leadership in the future.

It is also important to understand other influences on culture – what are the limits on leader control and influence and how can they best negotiate those influences? Within the context of continuous transformation and the emphasis on joint CF approaches to operations, it is increasingly important to develop integrated and complementary strategies to enhance understanding of unique CF sub-cultures, to make relevant comparisons across sub-cultures, and to increase understanding of how various aspects of culture become embedded within various sub-cultures, as well as across the institution.

The development of strategy to meet the changing demands of the security environment is a significant undertaking for the CF. Increasingly, leading the institution means leading transformation and change on a continuous basis, as the life cycles of change initiatives keep getting shorter and shorter.[85] Leadership, at the institutional level in particular, is essentially about influencing the collective capacity of the organization,[86] in a way that leads to effective CF outcomes in five essential domains: mission success, military ethos and ideology, member well-being and commitment, internal integration, and external adaptability. The collective and integrated power of these domains is the favoured outcome; however, frequently these domains also represent competing values. Institutional leaders negotiate optimum outcome –

CF effectiveness. This demands expertise in understanding the multiple dimensions of influence that motivate people to make choices and act in particular ways. Institutional leaders are challenged to make distinctions between those aspects of the organizational culture that provide functional stability for the organization and its members, and those aspects which represent a barrier to effective change. This entails an understanding of the many influences on organizational culture, including those that are historical and persistent, and those that reflect contemporary Canadian and global society.

In an ideal state, the espoused strategy and ethos of the CF and the profession of arms has a direct relationship with the policies and practices developed and supported within the organization. However, the actual practices and the cultural influences driving those practices comprise a more realistic picture of the cultural resources available to leadership in implementing current direction and ensuring the success of strategies for the future. A network of institutional leaders situated across functional domains at the strategic and operational level, 'stewarded' by aligned institutional values and goals will provide an increased organizational capacity to ensure the success of all parts of the organization and the success of the institution within the context of continuous adaptation and change.

Stewardship of the profession and the cultures within is a significant and enduring challenge for leadership. All members of the profession of arms share in the responsibility for safeguarding the integrity, reputation, and image of the CF – at a minimum by regulating their personal conduct and by influencing others to comply with professional norms. As stewards of the profession, senior officers and NCOs have a particular obligation to shape and influence culture to ensure the continued legitimacy of the CF as a self-regulating national institution.[87]

SELECT BIBLIOGRAPHY

English, Allan D. *Understanding Military Culture: A Canadian Perspective*. Montreal & Kingston: McGill-Queen's University Press, 2004.

Harrison, Michael I. and Arie Shirom, *Organizational Diagnosis and Assessment: Bridging Theory and Practice*. Thousand Oaks: Sage, 1999.

Moskos, Charles C., John Allen Williams and David R. Segal, eds. *The Postmodern Military: Armed Forces After the Cold War*. New York: Oxford University Press, 2000.

Schein, Edgar H. *Organizational Culture and Leadership*. San Francisco: Jossey-Bass, 1985.

Sharpe, G. E. (Joe) and Allan D. English, *Principles for Change in the Post-Cold War: Command and Control of the Canadian Forces*. Winnipeg: Canadian Forces Training Materiel Production Centre for the Canadian Forces Leadership Institute, 2002.

Winslow, Donna, *The Canadian Airborne Regiment in Somalia: A Socio-cultural Inquiry*. Ottawa: Ministry of Public Works and Government Services, 1997.

ENDNOTES

1   Franklin C. Pinch, "Canada: Managing Change With Shrinking Resources" in Charles C. Moskos, John Allen Williams and David R. Segal (eds.) *The Postmodern Military: Armed Forces After the Cold War* (New York: Oxford University Press, 2000);

2   For detailed analysis of CF response to Somalia, see Bernd Horn, "An Absence Of Honour: Somalia – The Spark That Started The Transformation Of The Canadian Forces Officer Corps" ch. 10 in this volume, Allister MacIntyre and Karen D. Davis (eds.) *From the Canadian Forces Leadership Institute Research Files, Volume 1: Dimensions of Military Leadership* (Winnipeg: 17 Wing Publishing Office for the Canadian Defence Academy Press).

3   For overview of these and other issues as they impact change in CF see Pinch, "Canada: Managing Change With Shrinking Resources".

4   Canada. *Duty With Honour: The Profession of Arms in Canada* (Canadian Defence Academy, Canadian Forces Leadership Institute, 2003), Canada, *Leadership in the Canadian Forces: Doctrine* (Canadian Defence Academy, Canadian Forces Leadership Institute, 2005), and Canada, *Leadership in the Canadian Forces: Conceptual Foundations* (Canadian Defence Academy, Canadian Forces Leadership Institute, 2005). All available on-line at: http://www.cda-acd.forces.gc.ca

5   A 2004 bibliography includes over 170 references, dating from 1967 to 2004, close to 120 of which were written, published or presented from 1997 to 2004. Many are papers developed to satisfy the course requirements of senior officers attending the CF Advanced Military Studies, National Security Studies, and Command and Staff courses. See Shannen Murphy, *Annotated Bibliography: Culture in the Canadian Forces* (Ottawa, Canada: National Defence, Director Strategic Human Resources Research Note 04/04, 2004). A recent update to this work, expanded the bibliography to include the international literature with a specific focus on those sources discussing military culture, military organizational culture, organizational culture, or culture change; 16 sources, that directly address Canadian military culture, were identified. See Sam Alvaro, Samantha Urban, Brian McKee and Sarah A. Hill. *Military and Organizational Culture: An Annotated and Secondary Bibliography of Literature from the Past Ten Years* (Canada: Defence R&D Canada, Centre for Operational Research and Analysis Technical Memorandum 2005-43, 2005).

6   G. E. (Joe) Sharpe and Allan D. English, *Principles for Change in the Post-Cold War: Command and Control of the Canadian Forces* (Winnipeg, Canada: Canadian Forces Training Materiel Production Centre for the Canadian Forces Leadership Institute, 2002).

7   Canada, *Leadership in the Canadian Forces: Conceptual Foundations* (Canadian Defence Academy, Canadian Forces Leadership Institute, 2005), 98. Available on-line at: http://www.cda-acd.forces.gc.ca

8   Canada, *Leadership in the Canadian Forces: Doctrine*, p. 7.

9   Ibid., p. 11.

10   Ibid.

11   Canada, *Leadership in the Canadian Forces: Conceptual Foundations*, 19-21.

12   Canada, *Leadership in the Canadian Forces: Conceptual Foundations*, 129.

13   Edgar H. Schein, *Organizational Culture and Leadership* (San Francisco: Jossey-Bass, 1992) cited in *Leadership in the Canadian Forces: Conceptual Foundations*, 117.

14   For example, "Establish climate of respect for individual rights & diversity" is identified as a leading people function that contributes to the effectiveness dimension of military ethos. Canada. *Leadership in the Canadian Forces: Conceptual Foundations*, 49.

15   Canada, *Leadership in the Canadian Forces: Leading People* and *Leadership in the Canadian Forces: Leading the Institution* (Canadian Defence Academy, Canadian Forces Leadership Institute, in progress, 2006).

16   Canada, *Leadership in the Canadian Forces: Leading the Institution*, Chapter 1.

17   Canada, *Leadership in the Canadian Forces: Conceptual Foundations*, 115-117.

18   Richard Hagberg and Julie Heifetz, *Corporate Culture/ Organizational Culture: Understanding and assessment*, 2. http://www/hcgnet.com/html/articles/understanding-Culture.html. Accessed June 2005.

19   Edgar H. Schein, "Organizational Culture: What is it and how to change it" in Evans, P. and Doz, Y (eds.) *Human Resource Management in International Firms. Change, Globalization, Innovation* (London: MacMillan, 1989), 81.

20   Michael I. Harrison and Arie Shirom, *Organizational Diagnosis and Assessment: Bridging Theory and Practice* (Thousand Oaks: Sage, 1999), 263.

21   K. Lewin, R. Lippit & R. White, "Patterns of aggressive behaviour in experimentally created social climates" *Journal of Social Psychology*, Vol. 10, 271-299 cited in Daniel R. Denison, "What is the difference between organizational culture and organizational climate?"

22   Daniel R. Denison, "What is the difference between organizational culture and organizational climate? A naïve's point of view on a decade of paradigm wars" *The Academy of Management Review* 21 (1996), 635.

23   Kelly M. J. Farley, *A model of unit climate and stress for Canadian soldiers on operations.* (Ottawa, Ontario: Carleton University, Unpublished doctoral dissertation, 2002).

24   Role stress; work motivation; job satisfaction; psychological distress; quality of life; leadership style; confidence in leadership; cohesion; communication; climate; preparedness for deployment; perceived organizational support and organizational commitment; job performance; and retention/attrition intentions. The climate dimension includes dimensions of involvement, consideration, efficacy and fairness of rules; quality of feedback; autonomy and recognition/ encouragement derived from a questionnaire developed to examine

perception of Officer Cadets of the organizational climate at the Royal Military College of Canada. See M.Villeneuve and C. Gingras, "Report of the study of Officer Cadet's perception of the organizational climate at the Royal Military College of Canada" *American Journal of Community Psychology* 13, 693-713; and M. A. Riley, *Measuring the Human Dimension of Unit Effectiveness – The Unit Morale Profile* (Ottawa, Ontario: Director Human Resources Research and Evaluation Conference Paper 2002-01 presented at the 38th International Applied Military Psychology Symposium, 20-24 May 2002).

25   Denison, "What is the difference between organizational culture and organizational climate?"

26   Denison, "What is the difference between organizational culture and organizational climate?", 644.

27   Denison, "What is the difference between organizational culture and organizational climate?"

28   E. Jacques cited in Daniel R. Denison, "What is the difference between organizational culture and organizational climate? A native's point of view on a decade of paradigm wars" *The Academy of Management Review* 21 (1996), 619-654.

29   Daniel R. Denison, "What is the difference between organizational culture and organizational climate?

30   Ibid., 635.

31   Edgar H. Schein, *The Corporate Culture Survival Guide*. San Francisco: Jossey-Bass, 1999), 29.

32   Edgar H. Schein, *Organizational Culture and Leadership* (San Francisco: Jossey-Bass, 1985), 15.

33   Samuel P. Huntington, *The Soldier and the State: The Theory and Politics of Civil-military Relations* (Belknap Press of Harvard University, 1957).

34   Morris Janowitz, *The Professional Soldier: A Social and Political Portrait* (Glencoe, Ill: Free Press, 1960).

35   James Burk, "Military Culture" in Lester Kurtz and Jenifer E. Turpin (eds.) *Encyclopedia of Violence, Peace and Conflict* (San Diego, California: Academic Press, 1999).

36   Don M. Snider, "An uninformed debate on military culture" *Orbis* 43 (Winter, 1999), 6.

37   Edgar H. Schein, "Coming to a New Awareness of Organizational Culture", *Sloan Management Review* (Winter, 1984), 4.

38   Edgar H. Schein, *Organizational Culture and Leadership*, 15.

39   V. Sathe and E. J. Davidson, E.J. "Toward a new conceptualization of culture change", in Ahskenasy, N.M. Wilderom, C.P.M. and

Peterson, M.F. (eds.) *Handbook of Organizational Culture and Climate* (Thousand Oaks: Sage, 2000), 280.

40   Ibid., 280.

41   Edgar H. Schein, *The Corporate Culture Survival Guide.*

42   Edgar H. Schein, *Organizational Culture and Leadership.*

43   Joseph L. Soeters, Donna J. Winslow, and Alice Weibull, "Military Culture" in *Handbook of the Sociology of the Military* in Caforio, G. (ed.). (New York: Kluwer Academic, 2003.

44   S. Rutherford, S. "Organizational cultures, women managers, and exclusion" *Women in Management Review.* (16, 2001), 371–382. Rutherford, 2001: 372

45   Bolon, Donald S. and Bolon, Douglas S. 1994. 'A reconceptualization and analysis of organizational culture: The influence of groups and their idiocultures', in *Journal of Managerial Psychology.* 9 (5, 1994), 31.

46   Ibid., 31.

47   This summary list of roles adapted from Stephen P. Robbins and Nancy Langton *Organizational Behaviour, Concepts, Controversies, Applications*, 3rd Canadian Edition. (Toronto: Pearson Prentice Hall, 2003), 349.

48   Joseph L. Soeters et al, "Military Culture"

49   Don M. Snider, "An uninformed debate on military culture".

50   Ibid.

51   G. E. (Joe) Sharpe and Allan D. English, *Principles for Change in the Post-Cold War: Command and Control of the Canadian Forces*, vi.

52   Don M. Snider, "An uninformed debate on military culture", 6.

53   Ibid., 6.

54   Ibid., 7.

55   Colonel Mike Capstick, "Defining the Culture: The Canadian Army in the 21st Century", in *Canadian Military Journal* (Spring, 2003), 51.

56   Joseph L. Soeters et al, "Military Culture", 246.

57   *Military HR Strategy 2020: Facing the People Challenges of the Future.* P. 20

58   Lieutenant-Colonel John Girard. 2004. "Defence Knowledge Management: A Passing Fad?" *Canadian Military Journal.* Vol. 5, No. 2 (Summer 2004): 17-27.

59   See, for example, Donna Winslow. 1997. *The Canadian Airborne Regiment in Somalia: A Socio-cultural Inquiry* (A study prepared for the Commission of Inquiry into the Deployment of Canadian Forces to Somalia). Ottawa, Canada: Minister of Public Works and Government Services Canada.

60 See Stella M. Nkomo and Taylor Cox Jr., "Diverse Identities in Organizations" *Handbook of Organization Studies* (London: Sage Publications, 1996), 338-356.

61 Gail Zellman, J. Z. Heilbrun, C. Schmidt, C. and C. Builder, "Implementing policy change in large organizations" in *Sexual Orientation and US Military Personnel Policy: Options and assessments* (Washington: RAND, National Defence Research Institute MR-323-OSD 1993), 369.

62 For US sources see Don Snider, "An uninformed debate on military culture"; M. Williamson, "Does Military Culture Matter"; J. Hillen, J. "Must US Military Culture Reform?" *Orbis* 43 (Winter, 1999), 14-26; and for UK sources see C. Dandeker, J. Higgs, F. Paton, and J. Ross, J. *The Future of British Military Cultures. London: British Military Studies Group,* 1997).

63 Chief Review Services and the Royal Military College of Canada. 1999. "General Officer Statement of Expectations" in *General Officers Ethics Focus Session #3,* Co-sponsored by Major-General K.G. Penney, Chief Review Services, NDHQ and Brigadier-General K. Hague, Commandant, Royal Military College of Canada. 8 July 1999.

64 See Nicholas Abercrombie, Stephen Hill and Bryan S. Turner. 2000. *The Penguin Dictionary of Sociology* (Fourth Edition). London: Penguin Books.

65 George Elliott Clarke. 1998. "Contesting a Model Blackness: A Meditation on African-Canadian Americanism, or The Structures of African Canadianite." *Essays in Canadian Writing,* 63 cited in Liane Curtis, Dipti Gupta and Will Straw. 2001. "Culture and Identity: Ideas and Overviews" paper commissioned by the Department of Canadian Heritage.

66 Allan D. English, *Understanding Military Culture: A Canadian Perspective* (Montreal & Kingston: McGill-Queen's University Press, 2004).

67 W. R. Kelley, *A Study of Attitudes Toward Military Service: Sub-cultural Influences* (Willowdale, Ontario: Canadian Forces Personnel Applied Research Unit, Research Note 67-2, 1967).

68 Leadership instability was concerned with the rate of individual leader rotation. The report noted "the stability of individuals in unit leadership roles, and thus the relationship between the leaders and the led is critical to the development of trust and confidence" Ibid., 37.

69 Ibid.

70 C. A. Cotton, *Military Attitudes and Values in the Army in Canada.*

(Willowdale, Ontario: Canadian Forces Personnel Applied Research Unit, 1979), 6.

71   Ibid., 9.

72   Ibid.

73   Donna Winslow, *The Canadian Airborne Regiment in Somalia: A Socio-cultural Inquiry.* (Ottawa: Ministry of Public Works and Government Services, 1997).

74   As the Canadian Airborne Regiment (CAR) drew their members from combat arms units across the CF, the extent to which the problems were isolated to CAR has been debated. See, for example, Bernd Horn, "An Absence Of Honour: Somalia – The Spark That Started The Transformation Of The Canadian Forces Officer Corps".

75   For discussion of 'Uncovering the Levels of Culture' see Edgar H. Schein. *Organizational Culture and Leadership*, 16-27.

76   English, *Understanding Military Culture: A Canadian Perspective.*

77   Mike Capstick, Kelly Farley, Bill Wild and Mike Parkes. *Canada's Soldiers: Military Ethos and Canadian Values in the 21st Century* (Ottawa, Ontario: National Defence, Director General – Land Capability Development, Land Personnel Concepts and Policy, 2005).

78   Ibid., 70.

79   Ibid., 70.

80   Ibid., 47.

81   Ibid., 2.

82   Brian McKee, *Organizational Culture: Towards the Development of a Strategy for the Study of Cultural Change within the Canadian Forces* (Ottawa, Canada: National Defence, Director Strategic Human Resources & Social Science Operational Research Team Research Note 10/04, 2004).

83   Brian McKee and Sarah A. Hill. *The "How To" of Organizational Culture Change in the CF* (Canada: National Defence, Centre for Operational Research and Analysis, In Progress).

84   Allan D. English. 2004. *Understanding Military Culture: A Canadian Perspective.* Montreal & Kingston: McGill-Queen's University Press.

85   Hubert Saint Onge. 2005. *Organizational Transformation…leading to accelerate change.* Presentation given to ADM (HR-Mil) Strategic HR Conference on Culture. Ottawa. 28 February 2005.

86   See Stuart A. Beare. 2002(?),Paper written in partial fulfillment of course requirements for Canadian Forces College, National Security Studies Course 3.

87   *Leadership in the Canadian Forces: Conceptual Foundations*

CHAPTER THREE

THE CANADIAN DEFENCE PROFESSIONAL

Dr. Bill Bentley

In Canadian civil-military relations there has always been a close relationship between civilian officials and senior military officers. This is not to say that there is not a healthy tension between the civilian perspective and the military. There always was – and sometimes it was intense – most recently, for example, during the Somalia Affair in the mid-1990s. However, there was always a good understanding that at the policy-strategy interface, primarily in Ottawa, that each component was dependant on the other if the defence mission was to be accomplished.

Nonetheless, until recently, the two spheres – civilian and military – were maintained quite separately. Until the 1972 Re-organization Act integrated the two spheres in a single NDHQ this separation was physical, organizational as well as cultural. Since 1972, the two were thoroughly blended with the CDS heading the CF and the DM heading the civilian component of the department. In keeping with the role of the DM in any government department, however, the DMs political and financial responsibilities extended throughout both components of the Department of National Defence.

Despite the integration of headquarters the cultural gap between career public servants and professional military officers was never closed. Military officers always felt that the civilians did not understand the true nature of conflict and war and were constantly thwarting efforts to obtain the required resources. Frequently, they viewed their civilian counterparts as mere mouthpieces for whatever political party was in power. For their part, public servants felt that the military, constantly in transit through NDHQ, did not understand the complexities of policy-making in the context of the Federal system, could not master the intricacies of "working the town" on behalf of DND and the CF and, in fact, did not understand the constitutional responsibilities of the Public Service of Canada. For the most part, both perspectives reflected a great deal of truth.

Civil-military relations evolved during the Cold War in a particular political-strategic context. In the Canadian case, it was prosecuted in a multilateral context anchored on the UN, NATO and NORAD. Forward deployed forces occupied static positions in Europe and Canada and prepared to fight a very dangerous but nonetheless, set-piece battle. Canadian military forces deployed on UN missions operated under the operational control of the UN and had minimal contact with their foreign affairs colleagues operating from diplomatic missions around the world. Contact with aid officials and NGOs was more frequent but such interaction was ad hoc and definitely not integrated.

In Ottawa, the complex but slow moving dynamics of defence planning and procurement created an environment that was favourable to bureaucracy and management. Because planning and directing strategy took place in the context of potential operations and because the forces in question were always under somebody else's strategic and operational control, an operational orientation or spirit was often lacking. Stability evolved into inertia and increasingly there developed an institutional focus rather than an operational one.

In this environment, a pervasive and counter-productive dynamic evolved. One in which the military component advocated, albeit in a low-key manner, that the two components of headquarters should be separated. Organizationally, the Department should go back to the "good old days" pre-1972. Civilian officials, on the other hand felt that only strict civilian control over the military could curtain their strategic flights of fancy and the influence of both NATO and the US theory and doctrine on Canadian military thinking.

The end of the Cold War radically changed the context in which civil-military relations were prosecuted. This ended a particular era of Canadian civil-military relations; although both communities were slow to realize this fact. Initially, the combination of severe budget cuts alongside a virtual explosion in operational tempo actually exacerbated tensions between civilians and the military. The overall fall-out of the Somalia affair leading the Minister's Report to the Prime Minister in April 1997 focused everyone's attention on the need for reform and a new approach to civil-military relations. The terror attack in New York on September 11, 2001 completed the paradigm shift in the security environment and Canadian forces deployed on their first combat mission since the Korean War.

The new situation was acknowledged politically in 2004 with the promulgation of Canada's first explicit National Security Policy, followed in 2005 with the first Defence Policy Statement since 1994. At the strategic level, a new CDS was appointed. CDS General Hillier launched the CF Transformation Project. Transformation was to be guided by six principles. Principle number 5 was to move "from an institutional focus to an operational focus". Principle number 6 was: "towards viewing the regular and reserve components, including the public service, as part of a single solution". Taken together, these principles represented an explicit recognition that both components of the DND/CF needed to adjust their mind-sets and devise a model and methodology to bring about the required "single solution". Thus arose the concept of the defence professional; that is to say a Public Servant working in DND with an acute sense of their responsibilities to directly support operations. This support would now extend to the actual deployment of civilian officials and employees into theatres of operation. Such employment at the tactical level could range from technicians upwards to senior level Public Servants. At the same time for the concept to work the military component would have to recognize the validity of the concept and make their own adjustments additionally, culturally and in terms of operational doctrine to bring about the required integration.

CONTEXT

Before addressing a methodology and model to realize the concept of a defence professional, it is necessary to clearly understand what has changed in the character of conflict and war that demands this new approach.

The Prussian military theorist Carl von Clausewitz demonstrated in *On War* that the nature of war does not change. In his recent book, *Another Bloody Century: Future Warfare* (2005), the noted strategic theorist, Colin S. Gray echoed the same thought 175 years later when he argues that "*war is war, in all periods,* of all kinds, between all manner of belligerents, and regardless of the contemporary weaponry and tactics". However, Gray also agrees with Clausewitz that the character of any particular war or conflict varies enormously throughout history. As Clausewitz observed "we wanted to show how every age had its own kind of war, its own limiting conditions and its own peculiar preconceptions. Each period, therefore, would have held its own theory of war".

By all accounts we are entering a new era of war, one that differs markedly from the last 200 years. To see this, we need to understand the difference between war and warfare and have an appreciation for the General System of War and Conflict. In the former case, war is a relationship between belligerents, not necessarily states. Warfare is the conduct of war, primarily, though not exclusively, by military means. The two concepts are not synonymous. There is more to war than warfare. Structurally, this is reflected in the fact that in the General System of War and Conflict, wars and conflict are conducted at four levels –political, strategic, operational (theatre) and tactical – with each level sitting within the context of the other (nested), in descending order from the political. It is this that gives shape to all of the activities of all the levels aimed at the same objective, and enables coherence between them. War, therefore, is the totality of the System led by policy. Warfare is conducted at the other three levels with strategy acting as the bridge between the two concepts. As Clausewitz maintained, warfare has its own grammar but not its own logic. The logic is supplied by policy.

In terms of the models of the General System of War and Conflict, war can be of two kinds – unlimited and limited. Napoleonic war, WWI, WWII and potentially the Cold War are examples of the former. The total defeat of the opponent and unconditional surrender were the goals. The latter sets more limited objectives such as what was seen in the case of Korea. There are two strategic systems that correspond to these types of war. In the case of unlimited war, the objective is decisive military victory over the enemy. The strategy is one of annihilation. With limited war such a goal is not necessary, nor in fact, desirable. In such a bi-polar strategy, the goal is pursued on two poles, simultaneously and/or sequentially, one the battle pole, the other the non-battle pole. To be effective, these two poles must be completely integrated at the strategic, operational and tactical levels. At the same time, it must be appreciated that campaigns at the operational level can be as large and intense on the bi-polar strategy as they are in the strategy of annihilation. The campaign in 1990-1991 in the Gulf War is a good example of this fact. Similarly, battles on the battle pole at the tactical level will be violent, deadly and oriented on the destruction of elements of the opponent.

War, warfare and conflict conducted in accordance with the bi-polar strategy leads logically and directly to the so-called "three-block war" at the tactical level. In a "three block war" military professionals often literally find themselves distributing aid on one block, acting as interposed peacekeepers on the second block and finally, engaged in armed conflict on the third. In this scenario civilian officials will frequently be intimately involved in activities on the first two blocks, sometimes even in charge of them. The two poles of a bi-polar strategy are directed from the strategic level and integrated at the operational level in the theatre of operations. Activities on these two levels, in a bi-polar strategy, must produce campaigns that successfully integrate defence, diplomacy and development.

In order to understand the new era of war and warfare it is useful to view the subject in terms of "generations of war," a concept first postulated by the American ex-Marine and current military analyst William Lind. According to this view we are now in an era of 4th generation war (4GW). The modern era dawned in terms of 1st generation war, based on massed manpower. This era is exemplified by the Napoleonic period. With the advent of early industrialization, the world, or at least the west, entered the era of 2nd generation war or warfare based on massed firepower. This era culminated in the First World War. Advanced industrialization and the desire to avoid the slaughterhouse of the First World War led to the development of 3rd generation war based on massed manœuvre. This was first demonstrated in World War II and was the prevailing paradigm throughout the Cold War. These three "generations" of war can be characterized as the industrial war/warfare model. Essentially, industrial war sought decisive military victory and ultimately culminated in taking the people themselves as the target as the carpet-bombing in WWII and potential widespread nuclear destruction in the Cold War illustrate. Industrial war was conducted in accordance with the strategy of annihilation.

Fourth generation warfare evolved out of the radically different conditions of the post-Cold War era. It is not a war of conquest or territory. The enemy is not a nation-state and its people. It is a type of war involving insurgencies, terrorist acts and ideas. It is as General Sir Rupert Smith says in his book the *Utility of Force: the Art of War in the Modern World,* "war amongst the people", not against the people. In *The Pentagon's New Map,* Thomas Barnett refers to 4GW as "war in the context of everything else."

The paradigm of 4GW reflects a very different world from the one of industrial warfare. It is one in which the political and the military are both parts of the same continuum, often working together. And this applies throughout all levels of the General System of War and Conflict, down to and including the tactical. This latter phenomenon is a radical departure from the character of war and warfare in earlier eras. Civilian agencies, of course, do not take part in military action on the battle pole, though military representatives may be part of non-military activities on the non-battle pole. The political-military relationship is both more complex than in industrial war and absolutely crucial in ensuring a successful outcome.

Overall, therefore, if a decisive strategic victory was the hallmark of interstate, industrial war, establishing a condition may be deemed the hallmark of the new paradigm of 4GW. In other words, modern military operations are dealt with as one amongst many activities of states and may have to be sustained almost endlessly. As Marine Colonel D. Hemmes concluded in his study of 4GW, *The Sling and the Stone*, 4GW is measured not in months or years, but in decades. Returning to General Sir Rupert Smith, "unlike industrial war, in war amongst the people, no act of force will ever be decisive; winning the trial of strength will not deliver the will of the people, and at base that is the only true aim of any use of force in our modern conflict."

Canada is committed to waging 4GW in this age of failing and failed states, regional instability and terrorism. Bosnia was our first full-scale encounter with this form of conflict and now Afghanistan poses the classic challenge. Not only must military and civilian officials work seamlessly tighter at the political-strategic level, each sharing a comprehensive understanding of the nature of modern conflict; but, this co-operation must extend through the operational level at CEFCOM, Canada Com, SOFCOM and Operational Support Command, to the tactical level in Kandahar and the Provincial Reconstruction Teams. This template will undoubtedly be repeated in other conflicts in the future.

THE DEFENCE PROFESSIONAL MODEL

How then does Canada produce the "single solution" demanded by the new security environment and directed by the chief of the Defence Staff? The foundation must be built on a sound conceptual basis and this basis is the concept of professionalism and professional ideology.

Out of the torment of the 1990s came the realization that Canadian military professionalism had been eroded. This was forcefully argued in the Somalia Commission report,

Dishonoured Legacy, and courageously acknowledged in the *Minster's Report to the Prime Minister* in April, 1997. A process was set in motion thereafter first in the Office of the Special Advisor to the Chief of the Defence Staff and then at the CF Leadership Institute to examine closely the concept of military professionalism. The intent was to define, describe and explain the desired nature of Canadian military professionalism and the result was *Duty With Honour: The Profession of Arms in Canada* promulgated under the signatures of the Governor General, the Minister of National Defence and the Chief of the Defence Staff. A similar process needs to be conducted to establish the nature of the Canadian civilian defence professional within the context of the wider Public Service.

The concept of a profession comprises five elements:

1. Specialized work grounded in a body of theoretically based, discretionary knowledge and skills;

2. Exclusive jurisdiction controlled by occupational negotiation with both the government and other stakeholders in society;

3. A sheltered position in society labour markets based on qualifying credentials;

4. A formal training program, controlled by the occupation and associated with higher education; and,

5. Greater commitment to good work, not economic gain and quality rather than efficiency.

Professions, therefore, are often described in the relevant scholarly literature as:

"...an exclusive group of people who possess and apply a systematically acquired body of knowledge derived from extensive research, education, training and experience. Members of a profession have a special responsibility to fulfill their function competently and objectively for the benefit of society.

Professional are governed by a code of ethics that establishes standards of conduct wile defining and regulating their work. This code of ethics is enforced by the members themselves and contains values that are widely accepted by society at large."

Based on this general definition, the Canadian military professional is defined in terms of four attributes based on its function for the ordered application of military force in accordance with government direction. These are responsibility, expertise, identity and professional ideology.

Responsibility derives from two imperatives – societal and function. First, the profession is responsible to protect Canadians and promote Canadian interests while remaining reflective of Canadian society and subordinate to civilian authority. Second, it is responsible to maintain the profession to the highest level of defence capability and operational readiness. It must be "fit to fight."

Expertise comprises the full, wide range of knowledge and skills necessary to enable mastery of the battlespace across the spectrum of operations. This expertise is differentiated throughout the organization of the Canadian Forces.

The military profession is acutely aware of its unique place and role in society as members of the Canadian Forces. Internally, there is a hierarchy of identities that ascends from branch to environment to the CF, Canada and the rule of law. Finally, professional ideology claims a specialized, theory-based body of knowledge authoritative in both a functional and cognitive sense and a transcendental value that adjudicates how the knowledge is applied.

This latter attribute forms the core of Canadian military professionalism. The unique theory-based knowledge is, in fact, the General System of War and Conflict discussed earlier. Members progressively acquire knowledge at each level – tactical, operational, strategic and civil-military relations. The transcendental value in question is the Canadian military ethos.

Eliot Freidson, who has spent a full career as a scholar studying professions, compares professional ideology to the ideology of the market, or entrepreneurialism, and to bureaucratic ideology, or managerialism. Each of these ideologies treats and manages knowledge differently than professions and claim an ethic substantially different than professional ethics or military ethos. Either can be anathema to professionalism if they are allowed to erode professional ideology. Thus, for example, the ex-CDS General G. C. E. Theriault opined that, "The military sometimes reflects some of the worst characteristics of bureaucracies: a focus predominantly on internal structures and interests, with a commensurate detachment from external factors and the larger community. It has great difficulty in differentiating between its own interests and the interests of the state, viewing both as coincident when, in fact, they are often quite different."[1]

The Canadian military ethos itself comprises three components – Beliefs and Expectations About Military Service, Fundamental Canadian Values and Core Military Values. The Beliefs are unlimited liability, fighting spirit, teamwork and discipline. Fundamental Canadian Values are derived from the Charter of Rights and Freedoms and the Core Military Values are Duty, Loyalty, Integrity and Courage.

In the final analysis the Canadian military profession is defined in Duty With Honour as follows:

> "The profession of arms in Canada is composed of military members dedicated to the defence of Canada and its interests as directed by the Government of Canada. The profession of arms is distinguished by the concept of service before self, the lawful, ordered application of military force and the acceptance of the concept of unlimited liability. Its members possess a systematic and specialized body of military knowledge and skills acquired through education, training and experience and they apply this expertise competently and objectively in the accomplishment of their mission. Members of the Canadian profession of arms share a set of core

values and beliefs found in the military ethos that guides them in the performance of their duty and allows a special relationship of trust to be maintained with Canadian society."

The Canadian profession of arms is an inclusive one made up of officers and NCOs as well as the Primary Reserve. The Chief of the Defence Staff is the Head of the Profession of Arms in Canada.

There is no doubt that the Canadian Public Service is a professional institution comprised of professional Public Servants. As described in *A Strong Foundation: Report of the Task Force on Public Service Values and Ethics* (1996), "A professional Public Service implies three things: a body of knowledge, skills and expertise that those outside of the profession are unlikely to possess; a set of values and attitudes that determine the culture of the profession; and, a set of standards for both of these. Some length of time is normally required to gain the knowledge, skills, sensitivities and outlook the profession requires. Some significant portion of life is usually devoted to acquiring the intellectual and moral capital to perform at a high level of professional competence."

The Clerk of the Privy Council is the professional head of the Public Service.

Somewhat analogous to the Canadian profession of arms, the Public Service struggled with the nature and status of its professionalism throughout the 1990s and into the new century. In 1989, the government introduced *Public Service 2000 (PS 2000)*, a process to reform and renew the Public Service by making it less rule bound and more innovative, focused on achieving results and serving the public. A new management philosophy would decentralize authority and emphasize developing skills and potential staff. *PS 2000* reflected a profound belief that private sector management techniques were superior to public sector techniques that they could work in government and should be introduced to government operations as quickly as possible.

According to Donald Savoie, the vocabulary in government was transformed in the 1990s. "It is safe to assume that career officials who served earlier would have had difficulty identifying with it. Politicians and senior officials set out to change government into business units. Strategic plans gave way to business plans and performance pay would become a major element in compensation. The new vocabulary also served notice to career officials that their political masters had a new role for them – the hard-nosed business manager."(Breaking, p.96)

Management was perceived to be a skill quite independent of the subject matter being managed, and managers could be transferred to completely different economic or social programmes. If managers had the skills and access to the necessary data, they could, it was thought, run anything. At the same time, new service delivery techniques adopted values that were more characteristic of the private sector and that conflicted with traditional Public Service values. Clearly, somewhat similar to the situation in the Canadian profession of arms, bureaucratic ideology and the ideology of the market threatened to undermine the professional ideology of the traditional Public Service.

PS 2000 did not solve the problems it was intended to address and, in 1996, the Clerk of the Privy Council introduced a new initiative, *La Releve*. It was designed to deal with a perceived crisis in leadership and to address widespread malaise in the Public Service that had not been assuaged by the measures introduced in *PS 2000*. According to the Auditor-General, in *Reflections On A Decade Of Serving Parliament: Report of the Auditor General of Canada to the House of Commons* (2001) however, *La Releve* appeared to have died the same quiet death as *PS 2000*. Furthermore, the Auditor-General reported that the reform of the Public Service advanced little over the 1990s. The efforts of several generations of well-meaning senior officials to streamline and modernize the Public Service have been stymied by the tangles of roles and responsibilities of the institutions that manage the Public Service and by the legislative framework that applies. A 1998 survey publication, "*The View From*

Here," reflecting the views of 30,000 mid-level Public Service managers reported continuing cynicism, embitterment and lack of trust.

The difficulties encountered in reforming the professional Public Service compound the problem of defining the civilian defence professional. Even with a strong, vibrant Public Service the challenge of differentiating a small sub-set of the approximately 146,000 Public Servants serving in line departments is a difficult proposition. Unlike the CF, where uniform members never leave the institution, Public Servants in DND often move to other departments and Agencies. Some return, others don't. To be sure, many spend most, if not all, their career in the Department of Defence. These latter officials must form the core of the defence professional community. However, the concept must have a much wider currency throughout the Public Service. Any model that purports to represent a civilian defence professional, therefore, needs to take account of the complexity of the whole Public Service structure and its Human Resources management processes.

Having acknowledged the problem, the issue is to describe a model of professionalism for the Public Service, how that model will have to modified to accommodate the unique requirements of a defence professional and finally how this modified model can be linked closely to the profession of arms model. Using the generic model of the profession of arms we can define the Public Service professional in terms of the same four attributes – responsibility, expertise, identity and professional ideology.

In terms of responsibility, in the heart of most Public Servants lies the conviction that service to the public, the public good or to the public interest is a responsibility that makes their profession like no other. It is important to realize, however, that the responsibility of Public Servants is tied solely to the government of the day. Although they should never be asked to do something unlawful, they have an unconditional duty to serve the minister loyally. Consequently, Public Servants are servants of the Crown. The

PCO published a document in 1990 on the role and responsibility of career officials. (*Notes on the Responsibility of Public Servants in Relation to Parliamentary Committees*) It states that it is the responsibility of individual Public Servants to provide advice and information to ministers, to carry out faithfully the directions given by ministers, and in so doing serve the people of Canada. Public Servants are accountable to their superiors and ultimately to their minister for the proper and competent execution of their duties. Responsibility for providing information to Parliament and its committees rests with the minister. When Public Servants appear before committees they appear on behalf of their minister. Career officials have no higher obligation to Parliament.

In terms of expertise, the necessary knowledge and skills differentiate widely throughout the Public Service, and encompass a large number of disciplines according to where the individual is employed throughout all departments, agencies and other organizations in federal government.

The Public Service, as a corporate body, certainly has a unique identity associated with its responsibility to serve the public good. Generally, Public Servants are acutely aware that this means as a body they serve the sitting government. Also, like the military there is a distinct entry process and the Public Service largely self-regulates, setting and maintaining professional standards themselves.

In terms of professional ideology, the Public Service does claim a body of specialized knowledge unique to itself as a professional institution. This claim rests primarily on a special understanding of how "government and Canadian politics work." The claim is based heavily on an experiential component, although training and education are also important to sustaining the claim. The widely recognized body of systematic, theory-based knowledge is made up of Public Administration, Theory of Government, Canadian Politics, General Management Theory, Human Resources Management, Policy Planning and Decision-making theory. This is a rather amorphous body of expertise, much of it common to several other fields of endeavour. It therefore renders the public service profession vulnerable to the corrosive influence of bureaucratic ideology and the ideology of the market (entrepreneurialism). It is the role of professional ideology to contain this threat.

The transcendental value in question, analogous to the Canadian military ethos, is the Public Service Code of Ethics. The Public Service Code of Ethics comprises a family of values:

The Democratic Values of: Responsible Government, Rule of Law, Support of Democracy, Loyalty, Respect for Authority of Elected Officeholders, Neutrality-Non-Partisanship, Accountability, Due Process and the Public Good.

The Professional Values of: Neutrality, Merit, Excellence, Effectiveness, Economy, Frankness, Objectivity and Impartiality of Advice, Speaking Truth to Power, Balancing Complexity, Fidelity to the Public Trust, Quality, Innovation, Creativity, Resourcefulness, Service to Citizens, Collaboration and Teamwork.

The Ethical Values of: Integrity, Honesty, Probity, Prudence, Impartiality, Equity, Selflessness, Discretion and Public Trust. The People Values of: Respect, Concern, Civility, Tolerance, Openness, Collegiality, Fairness, Moderation, Decency, Reasonableness, Humanity and Courage.

At the centre of this family of values is a set of implied core values. These core values are – service to Canadians, direct support to the government of the day and direct support to the minister.

To create the model of a civilian defence professional the Public Service professional construct needs to be modified, or customized, to incorporate those dimensions of professionalism peculiar to the attributes of expertise, identity and professional ideology that speak to the defence mission. This process, however, must not undermine the status of the individual as a full-fledged Public Service professional. Because of this, and of the utmost importance, the attribute of responsibility should not be substantially altered.

At the same time, to create the "single solution" called for in CF Transformation's Principle number 6, the CF military professional construct will also have to be modified as discussed below.

In terms of expertise, defence professionals must be introduced to, and in varying degrees educated about, the concept of the General System of War and Conflict. They will never be expected to be war-fighters, operational artists or military strategists but they must understand how each of these roles, at each level in the system (tactical, operational, strategic and policy) contribute to the defence mission. Such knowledge, important in itself to the performance of their duties, also enhances the mutual understanding and respect between defence professionals and their military colleagues. Within the context of the General System of War and Conflict, defence professionals will acquire a deep understanding of how each level, in general, is structured and practiced in the Canadian Forces.

In terms of professional ideology, the claim to a unique body of specialized knowledge will be altered from that of their colleagues throughout the rest of the Public Service. They will remain generalists in the sense that the Public Service has always called for; that is, employable in a wide range of roles and jobs across government, especially as they become more senior in rank and appointment. Nonetheless, as defence professionals, they now possess a theory-based body of knowledge quite distinct from anything contained in the wider professional ideology of the rest of the Public Service. This, of course, is that contained in the General System of War and Conflict.

When the other component of professional ideology – the military ethos and the "family of values" ethics of the Public Service - is compared, the strong basis for a "single solution is found in their common grounding in fundamental Canadian values. In addition, the common commitment to Canada and Canadians is critical to mutual understanding and respect. Beyond this, the values of teamwork and courage, common to both "ethics," form the basis for even closer union. Currently the Public Service value of courage speaks primarily to moral courage. In the future, in the context of 4th Generation Warfare, this value will have to reflect the concept of physical courage as well, at least for those defence professionals deployed into theatre at the operational and tactical levels of conflict. This perspective has always been an element of the code of values for members of the Foreign Service and CIDA but needs to play a more prominent role in the case of defence professionals deliberately employed alongside armed military professionals for prolonged periods in conflict zones.

The concept of discipline, found in the military ethos, will need to be introduced into the professional ideology of the defence professional. This does not mean military discipline *per se* but does require an understanding and acceptance of the need for responsiveness to orders and procedures essential to effectiveness and force protection in the field.

Taken together, these modifications to the professional ideology of the Public Service will forge an identity distinct from other sectors of the Public Service. Such an identity, of course, will bring the defence professional closer to their military colleagues, and will contribute immensely to the crucial ideas of unity of vision and unity of effort that, taken together, represent the "single solution" sought. This evolution will replace rhetoric with practice.

There are reciprocal modifications required in the military professional construct as well, if the context within which the defence professional is to fit is to be created.

In terms of expertise, there is a requirement for a much greater knowledge on the part of military professionals concerning the nature, structure and role of the Public Service in the Canadian constitutional political system. This knowledge is necessary to eliminate deeply ingrained attitudes on the part of many military personnel concerning how and why Public Servants serve Canada. This state of affairs was illustrated recently in a paper prepared by a senior officer attending the National Security Studies Course, the most senior professional development course in the CF. The author baldly states that the MND, the CDS <u>and to a lesser extent the DM</u>, all have responsibilities for the formulation and implementation of defence policy. (Emphasis added) In fact, while the CDS is the sole military advisor to the Government, the DM of Defence plays a much larger role in the area of <u>defence policy</u> than this statement implies.

In this author's opinion, more troubling still is this statement, very common amongst military professionals: "By defining the CF as Her Majesty's Forces and stipulating that all orders and instructions to the CF required to give effect to the decisions and directions of the Government or the MND shall be issued by or through the CDS, the NDA assigned a higher degree of trust and responsibility to the CDS than that of a Public Servant. Indeed, by making the Governor General the Commander-in Chief of the CF, it clearly split the responsibility of the CDS between the Minister on the one hand and the people of Canada on the other.

Beyond the fact that these statements are wildly inaccurate lies the belief system that continually threatens to poison relations between military and civilian members of the defence establishment.

With regard to the military's professional ideology, more attention needs to be paid to the field of civil-military relations, which is an integral part of the General System of War and Conflict found at the interface between policy and strategy. In a broader sense, of course, the military professional ideology certainly separates the military as a profession from all others. However, more attention to the commonality between the military professional and the defence professional will pay great dividends in pursuit of the "single solution" sought by both the CDS and the DM.

Now, how practical effect can be given to bringing together the two professional constructs is, indeed, a somewhat difficult issue. There remains a significant cultural gap between the two communities! There is a minimalist approach and a maximalist one. In the former case, introductory courses and seminars at entry and junior levels in both the military and civilian Public Servants entering the Department and the CF are necessary. Beyond that, attendance by mid-level and senior Public Servants from within the Department on such senior courses as the CF Staff College, The Applied Military Science Course, the National Security Studies Course and the Executive Leader Symposium (ELS) is also certainly desirable. The more programmed and systematic these measures can be made, the better. Nonetheless these actions fall far short of the ideal end-state of a distinct defence professional emerging within the context of the Public service and DND and such an individual being fully integrated into the "single solution" vision of CF Transformation.

The maximalist approach requires, first and foremost the active "championing" of the concept by both the DM and the CDS, within and without DND/CF. In the latter case, the DM will need to take the lead. The CDS, as "chief steward" of the profession of arms in Canada, will need to direct the actions necessary to modify the military professional construct in the ways outlined above. "Championship" of the concept will also have to be embraced as a priority for Chief of Military Personnel (CMP) and ADM (HR-Civ).

In doctrinal terms a couple of steps are required. First, the current Capstone doctrinal manual in the CF, *Duty With Honour: The Profession of Arms in Canada* should be re-issued in 2nd edition to address the subject of civil-military relations in more detail and introduce, and treat fully the concepts of professional ideology and the defence professional. Even before this action is completed, CMP and ADM(HR-Civ) should direct the production of a stand-alone doctrinal statement (manual?) concerning the defence professional and the "single solution." This would be a collaborative, consultative effort that could be led by the Canadian Forces Leadership Institute. The product would simply form a part of the suite of professional and leadership doctrine manuals already being promulgated – *Duty With Honour, Leadership in the Canadian Forces: Doctrine, Leadership in the Canadian Forces: Conceptual Foundations, Leadership in the Canadian Forces: Leading the Institution, Leadership in the Canadian Forces:*

Leading People and *Leadership in the Canadian Forces: Leading at the Operational Level of War and Conflict.*

Attendance on CF courses by civilian officials, including the senior courses being run at the Non-Commissioned Member Professional Development Centre at St. Jean, Que., should be increased dramatically. The curricula on these courses should be re-assessed to ensure that coverage of the role structure and practice of the Public Service is appropriate and that the concept of the defence professional is included. At the same time, military members, officers and NCMs, should attend appropriate Public Service courses, conferences and symposium to gain further insight into the nature and role of Canada's Public Service.

The current (and hopefully growing) practice of having civilians participate early and comprehensively in the training done at the operational and tactical levels in preparation for real-world deployments needs to be routine and mandatory. This builds trust, confidence, teamwork and mutual respect.

Finally, The CF has developed a Professional Development Framework (PDF) to guide professional development from entry to the most senior levels in the CF. This Framework is structured in four levels - junior, intermediate, advanced and senior. There are five meta-competencies that are addressed at each level – expertise, cognitive capacity, social capacity, change capacity and professional ideology. ADM(HR-Civ), working with the Canadian Defence Academy, should investigate how this Framework could be utilized within DND, complementing wider Public Service approaches and models, to structure professional development of civilian officials. Convergence on a common professional development model would be of great assistance in developing the desired defence professional and the "single solution" team.

As these measures are developed and implemented within DND/CF, consideration should be given to widening the concept of the defence professional to that of the "national security professional." This all-embracing concept would include, as a minimum, civilian officials from the PCO, the MND's Office, Foreign Affairs, CIDA, the Solicitor General's Department and others.

For the foreseeable future, war and conflict of a very complex and dangerous nature will remain a facet of the international system. Canada will, no doubt, continue to participate, in a multi-lateral way, in operations around the globe to seek stability and viable international relations. Such operations will be prosecuted in accordance with a bi-polar strategy, demanding the closest integration of military and non-military means and at all levels – tactical, operational and strategic. The type of co-operation required from NDHQ down to tactical operations in the field demands a cohesive, effective team of military professionals and civilian officials who are acutely aware of the demands imposed and who see themselves as defence professionals, fully capable of meeting the challenges of "war amongst the people."

SELECT BIBLIOGRAPHY

A Strong Foundation: Report of the Task Force on Public Service Values and Ethics. Government of Canada, 1996.

Bentley, L.W. *Professional Ideology and the Profession of Arms in Canada.* Toronto: CISS, 2005.

Canada, *Notes on the Responsibility of Public Servants in Relation to Parliamentary Committees.* Ottawa, Privy Council Office, Dec. 1990

Canada, *Results for Canadians: A Management Framework for the Government of Canada.* Treasury Board of Canada Secretariat, 2000.

Duty With Honour: The Profession of Arms in Canada. Government of Canada, 2003.

Forsey, Eugene. *How Canadians Govern Themselves*, Government of Canada, 2002.

Hodgetts, J.E. *The Canadian Public Service: A Physiology of Government, 1867-1970.* Toronto: University of Toronto Press, 1973.

Osbaldeston, Gordon. "The Public Servant and Politics," *Policy Options* 8, no. 1 (1987).

Reflections on a Decade of Serving Parliament. Report of the Auditor General of Canada to the House of Commons, February 2001

Savoie, Donald. *Governing From the Centre.* Toronto: University of Toronto Press, 1999.

--------- *Breaking the Bargain: Public Servants, Ministers and Parliament.* Toronto: University of Toronto Press, 2003.

Tellier, Paul. "Public Service 2000: The Renewal of the Public Service," *Canadian Public Administration* 33, no. 2 (Summer, 1990).

ENDNOTES:

1   Theriault, G. C. E., "Democratic Civil-Military Relations: A Canadian View", in Jim Hanson and Susan McNish, ed., *The Canadian Strategic Forecast 1996: The Military in Modern Democratic Society.* Toronto: CISS, 996, p.10.

CHAPTER FOUR

CANADA'S WAY IN WAR

Dr. Bill Bentley

The noted strategic theorist, Colin S. Gray, has recently written that war is a relationship between belligerents, not necessarily states. Warfare is the conduct of war, primarily, though not exclusively, by military means. The two concepts are not synonymous. There is more to war than warfare.[1] This reflects Gray's deep understanding that, as Clausewitz demonstrated in his magisterial work *On War*, "war is merely the continuation of a nation's policy with the admixture of other means."[2]

War is, therefore, a matter for politics and the policy level, whereas warfare is conducted at the operational and tactical levels. Strategy is the bridge between these two phenomena. It is the art of distributing and applying military means, or the threat of such action, to fulfill the ends of policy. Strategy is dynamic, iterative and non-linear. War should be viewed as a system with the sub-systems of strategy, operational art and tactics nested within the guiding system–policy.

Clearly then, to speak of "Canada's Way of War' goes beyond considering only the military component of national security policy and strategy, as important as this component is. In fact, in most states, the country's "way of war" is in part defined by the very nature of its civil-military relations and the tensions inherent in this aspect of national security. That is to say, the interface between policy and strategy, war and warfare. This is certainly no less true in the case of Canada. Therefore, in considering "Canada's Way in War" it is necessary to integrate the two concepts of war and warfare. That is, the way Canadians, as a nation, have understood war and conflict philosophically, culturally and politically and how the nation, mainly through its military instrument, has conducted warfare.

STRATEGIC CULTURE

A more precise way of analyzing the admittedly profoundly difficult issue of defining, describing and explaining any given nation's "way of war" is through the construct of strategic culture. Strategic culture refers to the socially transmitted habits of mind, tradition and preferred methods of operations that are more or less specific to a particular geographically based security community. It is a product of a particular national historical experience that has been shaped by a more or less unique, though not necessarily unvarying geographic context. Each strategic culture is inclined to erect what purports to be general theories on the basis of national historical experience and circumstances.

With this general understanding, the chapter defines strategic culture as follows:

> *An integrated system of symbols (argumentation structure, languages, analogies and metaphors, etc.) that acts to establish pervasive and long-term strategic preferences by formulating concepts of the role and efficacy of military force in political affairs. The strategic culture thus established reflects national preconceptions and historical experience as much as it does purely objective responses to any given threat environment.*

Strategic culture is a long-term, slow growth phenomenon not particularly dependent on specific individuals or even any single, significant event. In their book, The Making of Strategy, Williamson Murray et al argue that there are four major factors that contribute to the evolution of a strategic culture.[3]

1. Geography: The size and location of a nation are crucial determinants of the way policy-makers and strategists think about security and strategy. This, of course, includes all of the national resources available to the nation.

2. History: Historical experience influences strategic culture almost as strongly as geography.

3. Religion, Ideology and Culture. Taken together, these three terms comprise something the Germans have captured in a single expressive word – weltung schuung (world view or outlook on the world) the influence of this concept on strategic culture is both elemental and vast, according to Murray.

4. Governance: The structure of government and military institutions plays a crucial role in the development of strategic culture.

Colin S. Gray's own list is remarkably similar:[4]

1. Geography is the most fundamental of the factors that condition national outlooks on security problems and strategic solutions.

2. History

3. The influence of different national cultures upon choices for, and performance in, statecraft, war and warfare.

4. Relative technological competence is important. However, technicism refers to the disorder when that which is only technical displaces, and effectively substitutes for, that which has to be considered tactically, operationally and strategically in far more inclusive analysis.

To consider then, "Canada's Way in War" five factors, at a minimum should be analyzed: geography, history, culture, governance and technology. However, before turning to each of these factors in turn as they apply to Canada, there is an additional requirement to understand the generic structure of security problems and military operations that are addressed through the unique prism of a nation's strategic culture.

THE GENERAL SYSTEM OF WAR AND CONFLICT

Wars and conflicts in general are conducted at four levels – political, strategic, operational (theatre) and tactical, with each level nested or sitting within the context of the other in descending order from the political. It is this latter level that gives context to all the activities of all levels aimed at the same objectives and enables coherence between them.

Strategy is an expression of the aim and its links to the overall purpose and the context of the conflict, together with the limitations on action that flow from the political purpose, in the circumstances. It will describe the desired event pattern together with the measures intended to achieve this pattern, and it will allocate forces and resources. Analytically, there are essentially two strategic systems and they relate conceptually to the political purpose of the war or conflict. If the goal is very ambitious and requires the unconditional surrender of the opponent, then the strategy is one of decisive military victory or a strategy of annihilation. If, on the other hand, the goal is limited then the strategy is a bi-polar strategy, one pole being battle and the other, co-equal pole, being the simultaneous or sequential use of other non-military means to bring about a mutually satisfactory settlement. WWI and WWII are examples of the first strategic system while Korea would be a good example of the second. The suitability and/or utility of either type of strategy is very much the product of the strategic culture of the nation in question.

In Western military thought from the Napoleonic era through the 1990s, the strategy of annihilation was the foundational doctrine. To be sure, the British, French, Germans as well as the US fought limited campaigns and were extensively involved in policing their respective empires. However, every staff/war college curricula focused almost exclusively on how to fight major wars aimed at decisive victory. It was, in fact, a pervasive and powerful element in the strategic culture in all these nations. Only with the advent of nuclear weapons did the defence community throughout the Western world begin to explore fully the validity and implications of the alternate strategical system - the bi-polar strategy.

The theatre or operational level of war or conflict is conducted in the theatre of operations – a geographical area containing in its military and political totality an objective that, on achievement, alters the strategic situation to advantage. The theatre commander must make a plan, a campaign, which designates the path towards the final end-state and must orchestrate the activities of the whole command to achieve tactical objectives, which take the command as a whole in the designated direction.

Conceptually, at the operational level, warfare is conducted through either attrition or manoeuvre. Examples here might be the French in the interwar years with a doctrine of attrition that stressed firepower at the outset of a campaign, switching to manoeuvre only after the enemy had been thoroughly blooded. Conversely, the Germans devised a doctrine that stressed operational manoeuvre, preferring mass and mobility in the right proportions over mass firepower. For all operational level commanders the challenge is to get the right balance between mass and mobility – the definition of operational manoeuvre.

At the tactical level are engagements (military and non-military), battles and fights. The essence of all tactics is fire and movement. This is tactical manoeuvre. In essence it boils down to attrition by destruction. The basic tactical dilemma is to find the correct balance between how much effort to apply to striking the opponent to achieve the mission and how much to countering his blows and undermining his ability to sustain himself.

Canada's strategic culture addresses each of these levels in an interactive way in a manner unique to the country. All five factors, taken together, account for "Canada's Way in War" at each level.

STRATEGIC CULTURE: GEOGRAPHY

Canada's geography has always posed a particular dilemma. Initially, of course, membership in the British Empire and Britain's command of the sea reassured Canadians in security terms. By the turn of the 20th century, however, direct British support could no longer be counted on. At the same time, for as long as reasonably good relations could be maintained with the United States, geography seemed an almost insurmountable barrier to any direct military threat. At the same time, sharing a continent with a common border with such a powerful neighbor economically and culturally also posed a significant non-military threat in terms of national sovereignty and in extreme scenarios, actual absorption. Successfully maintaining good relations with the US also meant that Canada could rely on the militia paradigm throughout much of Confederation's history. This accorded well with historical experience and political preference (governance) up until WWII. WWI was a partial exception and, by 1917, the Canadian Army in Europe had to be seen as a battle-hardened, professional force. Nonetheless, the return to a very small standing force, ostensibly backed up by a large militia demonstrated Canada's political/ strategic preference very clearly.

Technology itself further complicated the matter with the advent of nuclear weapons and ballistic missiles. Now Canada was directly implicated in US security and a delicate balance was necessary between reassuring its American neighbor while still limiting the Canadian defence effort as much as possible under the circumstances. Thus, aerospace defence, and especially participation in NORAD, became priorities for Canadian defence policy.

Geography also conspired with history and culture to lead Canada to seek multi-lateral solutions to security/strategic problems in order to limit the influence of US preferences on Canadian policies. Over the years, Canada rather successfully maintained the required balance. Geography alone meant that a minimum defence effort had to be made, but ultimately such an effort gravitated toward something nearer to a diplomatic payment as opposed to a full-scale military response. With the demise of international communism, the potential for the influence of geography on Canada/US relations, and therefore Canada's strategic culture, to lessen was certainly there. However, the advent of global terrorism has reaffirmed the importance of geography in the shaping of strategic culture.

STRATEGIC CULTURE: HISTORY

Historical contingency in Canada's pre-Confederation era has contributed significantly to Canada's strategic culture. Under both French and English rule, the militia paradigm was entrenched in Canada. Furthermore, Canadian militiamen logically preferred to take the fight to the enemy rather than fight at home. Here, in embryonic form was the Canadian preference for expeditionary forces, usually small and only when required, rather than maintaining large standing forces at home.

After Confederation, the tension between involvement in European affairs, mainly British, and the progress towards autonomy and finally, full sovereignty was intense. There was a large and influential constituency in Canada, political military and social from before the First World War and extending well into the 1930s that called for close and large-scale support for the "Mother Country." This was largely provided for in World War One through the provision of the First Canadian Corps that established the reputation of Canadian soldiers for tactical excellence and fighting skills. However, after 1918, the political imperative for sovereignty together with the cost of developing the vast Canadian country meant that governments sought to limit military engagement with the Empire, reduce military spending to the lowest limit, and to restrict military to military co-operation between the Canadian military and the British to the maximum extent possible. This in itself was somewhat paradoxical since it was Canadian military prowess and the enormous sacrifices made in WWI that helped cement Canadian nationhood.

Growing political autonomy during this period brought with it a sense of international responsibility. Membership in the League of Nations was one response, although active involvement here was counter-balanced by a geographically induced sense of isolation and a continuing political preference for miniscule standing military forces and a large, but quiescent militia force. What military activity occurred was largely restricted to aide to the civil power in the 1920s, Depression era support for government programs and a great deal of military support for nation-building inside Canada itself. Significantly however, ever closer ties were developed on a military to military basis between the Canadian army and navy and their British counterparts. Thus, while the government sought to limit involvement in European affairs, military outlook and doctrine were heavily influences by British strategic concerns and doctrine. This would be a recurring theme in Canadian strategic culture with both the US and the ongoing debate of the primacy of either the UN or NATO in the post-WWII era.

World War II was certainly a turning point for Canada, politically, socially, economically and militarily. Over one million Canadians out of a population of 11 million served and served honourably. Canada's reputation for tactical excellence was consistently demonstrated. By the end of the war Canada was ready for full-scale international commitment first through the UN and then in 1949 by membership in NATO. Multilateralism became an entrenched cornerstone on Canadian foreign and defence policy with the concomitant requirement for relatively large military forces forward deployed and employed in Korea, briefly, Europe and a growing number of UN missions around the globe.

The threat of nuclear war between the Soviet Union and the US was the pre-eminent factor driving Canada's foreign and defence policy after WWII. Every effort was made to contribute to global stability unilaterally as in Canada's peacekeeping involvement in Vietnam or in a much larger way through the UN. Although humanitarian motives for extensive involvement in UN operations cannot be completely discounted; in fact, Canadian actions here were primarily to help rebuild US-UK relations, i.e., UNEF I in 1956 in the Middle East or to shore up NATO's southern flank through participation in UNFICYP in Cyprus. Stabilizing hot spots throughout the Cold War to minimize potential confrontations between NATO and the Warsaw

Pact largely account for Canada's continuing involvement in the Middle East, Africa and Kashmir.

It was however Canada's involvement on the ground in NATO that shaped the Canadian military doctrine during the whole period between the early 1950s and the early 1990s. Close ties with first the British in northern Germany and then the US in central Germany meant that Canadian military officers imbibed heavily in foreign strategic and operational theory and doctrine. In fact, a key element in "Canada's way of war" was most clearly manifested here. In addition to its multi-national nature, Canada's commitment was always restricted to the tactical level. Retrospectively, this had, of course always been the case since the Boer War, through WWI and WWII and Korea. This fact has two profound implications for Canadian strategic culture. First, little concerted thought was ever given to the operational level or operational art nor to applied military strategy or doctrine. At the same time, tactical elements were assigned to non-Canadian operational command in service packages – Navy to Navy, Army to Army and Air Force to Air Force. This led to a very distinct "strong single service" ideology, and its consequence would be felt significantly after the Cold War.

The heavy reliance on US, British and NATO doctrine at the operational and strategic levels meant that the Canadian military always viewed their tactical contributions as part of a strategy of annihilation. Despite extensive peacekeeping experience, curricula at the Canadian Staff Colleges and the National Defence College was dominated by doctrines that foresaw large-scale, high intensity warfare in which NATO sought decisive victory over the Warsaw Pact. At the theoretical and doctrinal levels there seemed little need to study bi-polar strategy.

With the demise of the Soviet Union and the consequent paradigm shift in the character of conflict and war in the 1990s the reliance on a strategy of annihilation was slowly eroded in US, British and NATO. It would take another 10 years for this process to have an appreciable impact in Canada and the Canadian Forces.

STRATEGIC CULTURE: RELIGION, IDEOLOGY AND CULTURE

This factor has had a strong influence on Canadian strategic culture in two important ways. As a liberal constitutional democracy, Canada always retained strong political ties with the both UK and the US, and indeed most western countries. Sharing a common ideology meant that Canada found any kind of totalitarianism anathema to the desired international order. Thus, it was a foregone conclusion that Fascism and Nazism would be resisted, although at what level remained a delicate political issue. Similarly, communism was to be contained and ultimately defeated. In the 20th century this lead to the raising and maintaining of large, standing professional forces in WWII and throughout the Cold War. In keeping with Canadian strategic preference and as an integral part of Canada's strategic culture, these forces were forward deployed in Germany. The strength of this factor, in practical terms, waxed and waned with the perception of the power of the competing ideology. Thus, during periods of détente, defence spending declined. Once the threat virtually disappeared, defence spending virtually plummeted. It remains to be seen whether the ideologies of ethnic extremism, Islamic fundamentalism and terrorism will continue to elicit a similar proactive response as earlier ideological challenges did.

However, by far the most important contribution this factor has made to strategic culture is the bi-cultural nature of Canadian confederation. It has been argued that peacefully managing English-French relations throughout Canada's history pre-disposes Canadian political culture to tolerance, mediation and patience. Consequently, so the argument goes, Canadians are "helpful fixers" on the international scene. In short, we make good peacekeepers! While not definitive, this line of thought is plausible. However, bi-culturalism helped to shape "Canada's way in war" in a much more direct way. Since an over-riding concern of Canadian political leaders since Confederation has been national unity, the threat of national disintegration was a paramount concern. French Canadian reluctance to wholeheartedly support the

British Empire in any significant military way from the Boer War onwards meant that military commitments had to be managed very carefully. The conscription crisis of WWI and WWII were salutary warnings of Canadian policy makers. The largely Catholic French Canadian population meant that support for anti-communism generally remained strong throughout the Cold War. The rise of separatism in the 1980s and 1990s complicated the matter further, and Canada's military involvement on any large scale anywhere remains subject to at least a careful survey of national attitudes and the English-French split on these matters. Certainly, it appears that strong Francophone objections to Canada's participation in the US-led invasion of Iraq were a significant factor in Federal decision-making.

Religion, ideology and culture in Canada also all coalesced around the issue of nuclear weapons. Canadians remained very ambivalent concerning their utility, and generally rejected the idea that Canada should ever become a nuclear weapons state. Although Canada did, in fact, possess such weapons in the 1950s and 1960s, they remained a burning political issue and were ultimately rejected.

The growing multi-cultural complexion of Canada since the 1960s has also helped alter and shape Canadian strategic culture. Whereas previously the Canadian focus strategically had always been on Europe, politicians increasingly have had to take into account Canadian attitudes towards instability and conflict virtually around the globe. Despite the slow growth nature of strategic culture this factor will invariably play a significant role in how Canada views security in the future.

STRATEGIC CULTURE: GOVERNANCE

There has always been a certain tension in Canadian civil-military relations. This is a characteristic of all western democracies, although the causes and remedies are unique to each. In Canada, these tensions have resulted in differing views on the utility of force in international politics and above all in the political desire to keep a tight control over military policy and defence spending at a minimum. If civilian policy-makers and officials seemed indifferent or unresponsive to perceived threats, military officers often appeared to civilians to be overly zealous in their demands for dealing with such threats. All would do well, however, to remember that in a liberal democracy the military can propose the level of armaments necessary to have a certain probability of being able to defend successfully against one's enemies, but only the civilian can say for what probability of success society is willing to pay. The military can describe in some detail the nature of the threat posed by a particular enemy, but only the civilian can decide whether to feel threatened and, if so, how, or even whether, to respond. The military assesses the threat, the civilian judges it.

In Canada's strategic culture these issues are addressed sporadically through the issuance of Defence White Papers (1947, 1964, 1970, 1987, 1994, 2004 and 2005) that set the context for political and bureaucratic processes to manage civil-military relations in the intervening periods. The establishment of the single Department of national Defence in the immediate aftermath of WWI was in large part a response to these considerations. Similarly, after the massive effort in WWII, measures were taken in the post-war years to re-establish tight political oversight and control spending. Unification and Integration were major governance decisions intended to shape the forces for rapid, expeditionary type operations and streamline the structure internally as well as reduce access to the Minister to one military officer, namely the new Chief of the Defence Staff.

These measures, however, actually did very little to reduce the "strong single service" ideology and at the same time perpetuated the practice of operating essentially only at the tactical level. At the end of the Cold War and throughout the 1990s, it became increasingly apparent that neither characteristic of the prevailing strategic culture was suited to the new challenges of global disorder and terrorism. The Defence White Paper of 2005 attempted to plot a new political-military course, and the CDS' Transformation Project was designed to implement this in detail. The first principle of transformation was to be moving from service culture to a CF culture. Structurally, for the first time in Canadian history, truly joint, operational level headquarters were established, and an explicit strategic staff organization was put in place. None of these steps flow naturally from Canada's extant strategic culture. They are progressive steps fully in accord with the battlespace of the 21st century. Nonetheless, the jury must remain out on how successful they will be when all the other dimensions of strategic culture are brought to bear.

STRATEGIC CULTURE: TECHNOLOGY

As an advanced industrial, now increasingly post-industrial nation, technology has always played an integral role in shaping Canada's strategic culture. However, perceptions of threat, the relatively small size of the military and constant downward pressure on defence spending has meant acquiring the most recent technology in sufficient quantity a problem. "Rust-out" and the "commitment-capability" gap are familiar phrases in the post WWII era. This has meant doing more with less but has also tended to avoid the worst excesses of technicism warned against by Colin Gray.

The concept of a Revolution in Military Affairs (RMA) plays a more direct and significant role in dramatically shaping a nation's strategic culture. Thus, the nuclear revolution has a dramatic effect on political-strategic doctrine in those countries that acquired these capabilities. By eschewing such weapons, itself a product of Canada's overall strategic culture, this revolution has had a more indirect and subtle effect in Canada. Similarly, for the time being at least, the movement into space has little real impact. Arguably, the revolution in information technology is, and will, have a greater impact. All associated technologies involving communications, precision weapons, sensors and weapons platforms reinforce the need for a better appreciation of joint operations and should tend to undermine the "strong single service" ideology, especially in the creation of joint, operational-level commands.

SUMMARY

When the interactive and interrelated factors contributing to Canada's strategic culture are considered holistically, what can be said by way of summary about "Canada's Way in War'? First, the primacy of policy and the subordination of the military to civilian control is an enduring characteristic of strategic culture deriving primarily from geography and history. Second, although somewhat muted by history and Canadian political ideology, Canada is not a nation of peacekeepers with a military force best suited for that role. The Canadian military was and is a combat capable force normally supported in that role by Canadian society. That we were actually quite good at peacekeeping is more a reflection of a strong professional ethic, including responsiveness to government direction, without shirking. Third, up to the present, the Canadian military has operated virtually exclusively at the tactical level, almost always in a multi-cultural context. This has profound implications for force structure, defence organization, military theory and higher-level doctrine. Finally, domestic influence on strategic culture has and will continue to be profound. Canadians can fight but prefer to be peaceable. They are militarily capable but also quite unmilitary. Canadians want to project Canadian values throughout the international system. Canada will therefore continue to operate in an expeditionary mode.

SELECT BIBLIOGRAPHY

Bentley, L.W. *Professional Ideology and the Profession of Arms in Canada.* Toronto: C.I.S.S., 2005.

Bland, Douglas. *Chiefs of Defence: Government and the Unified Command of the Canadian Armed Forces.* Toronto: C.I.S.S., 1995

--------- and Sean Maloney. *Campaigns for National Security: Canada's Defence Policy at the Turn of the Century.* Kingston: McGill-Queen's University Press, 2004.

Bothwell, Robert. *The Penguin History of Canada.* Toronto: Penguin, 2006.

Clausewitz, Carl von. *On War*. eds. Howard, Michael and Paret, Peter. Princeton: Princeton University Press, 1976.

Eayrs, James. *In Defence of Canada,* 5 vols. Toronto: University of Toronto Press, 1964-1983.

English, John. *Lament for an Army: The Decline of Military Professionalism*. Toronto: University of Toronto Press, 1998

Harris, Stephen. *Canadian Brass: The Making of a Professional Army, 1860-1939*. Toronto: University of Toronto Press, 1988.

Keating, Tom. *Canada and World Order*. Toronto: McClelland and Stewart, 1993.

ENDNOTES

1   Colin S. Gray, *Another Bloody Century: Future Warfare in the 21st Century.* Oxford: Oxford University Press, 2005, p.23.

2   Carl von Clausewitz, *On War* ed. Michael Howard and Peter Paret, Oxford: Oxford University Press, 1976, p. 8.

3   Williamson Murray, *The Making of Strategy.* Princeton: Princeton University Press, 1985, p. 14.

4   Colin S. Gray *Modern Strategy.* London: Weidenfeld, 1999, p.35.

CHAPTER FIVE

INSTITUTIONAL LEADERSHIP: UNDERSTANDING THE COMMAND, MANAGEMENT AND LEADERSHIP NEXUS

Colonel Bernd Horn

Undeniably, institutional leadership is critical to the well-being and success of an organization. It is at this level that leaders not only influence individuals but also the direction, efficiency and effectiveness of the organization. After all, institutional leaders are charged with overseeing system capabilities and performance and making major policy, system and organizational changes designed to ensure the organization's continued strength, relevancy and viability. They are responsible for creating and articulating the vision, as well as establishing the necessary strategies and sourcing the requisite resources to ensure its achievement. This often translates into changing institutional cultures and implementing enduring change. But, what it always entails is creating the conditions and the conducive environment necessary for operational success and Canadian Forces (CF) effectiveness – or simply put, leading the institution.

Undeniably, this is a tall order. The challenges of institutional leadership are enormous. They entail connecting with subordinates – convincing them, motivating them, and leading them – without the benefit of direct contact on a day-to-day basis. At lower levels (of CF rank and leadership) within the institution, leaders have the benefit of direct leadership that comes with "leading people." At this level, emphasis is placed on the unity of command – a concept that revolves around a single, clearly identified commander that is appointed for any given operation and who is accountable to only one superior. This ensures clarity and unity of effort, promotes timely and effective decision-making, and avoids conflict in orders and instructions. It is characterized by a clear chain of command, where command at each level is focused on one commander.

Furthermore, at this level as well, leaders exercise direct influence on individuals, teams, units and higher formations in the execution of operations and tasks. Leaders can lead by example in front of their troops – share hardship and experience and provide the on-site motivation and inspiration on a continuing and regular basis. Credibility, respect and buy-in are exponentially easier to achieve due to sheer presence and personal influence. Clearly, direct leadership can have an immediate effect on the ability, attitudes, behaviour, motivation and psychological states of individuals and groups, particularly during times of crisis or complexity.

Conversely, at the institutional level, the focus is less on unity of command and more on unity of purpose – the coordinated and cooperative effort by all individuals to successfully achieve a specified aim or set of objectives. At the institutional level there are many more external and uncontrollable factors that impact decision-making and what can actually be achieved. For instance, one cannot simply implement Quality of Life (QOL) enhancements – it becomes an exercise of seeking and securing approval from external agencies such as Cabinet, Treasury Board and other government departments. At this level, institutional leaders must often negotiate and build consensus through horizontal cooperation and networking. As already stated, philosophically and pragmatically, it is a dramatic shift from unity of command to unity of purpose.

As such, leadership at the institutional level depends on indirect influence. This refers to influencing others through the deliberate and reasoned modifications and alterations in the institution's organizational and environmental conditions (e.g. administrative policies, training programs and delivery, technology, organizational structures and procedures, etc...) that affect and shape attitudes, behaviours, capabilities and performance. After all, leadership at the institutional level is responsible for the overall long-term success of the organization by developing and maintaining the CF's strategic and professional capabilities and creating the conditions for operational success.

This translates into creating and articulating a clear vision that can permeate and resonate through all levels of an institution and attain the buy-in of all its members. It means convincing, inspiring, motivating, and leading subordinates in achieving that vision through concrete actions that demonstrate commitment, credibility and resolve. It entails removing the ambiguity, complexity and fear that inherently cloaks all change by explaining the vision, but more importantly, developing and articulating a clear plan of how to take the institution from where it is, to where it must be. It also means creating a governance structure to ensure that all conducted activities and efforts are in consonance with the vision and plan of action. Clearly, institutional leadership requires the courage and knowledge to take the institution to where it has to go.

Often adding to the challenge of institutional leadership is the misconception of the concepts of command, management and leadership. Paradoxically, these terms are often seen as synonymous, or mutually exclusive. It is this misunderstanding that can create a barrier to effective institutional leadership. In the end, one must understand the applicability, capability and relevance of an instrument to fully benefit from its use.

As such, it is important to begin with Command since it is the overarching concept. Command is the vested authority an individual lawfully exercises over subordinates by virtue of their rank and assignment. The NATO accepted definition, which has been adopted by Canada, defines command as "the authority vested in an individual of the armed forces for the direction, co-ordination, and control of military forces." Command is a very personal function and each person approaches it in different ways depending on their experience, circumstances and personality. Its essence, however, is the expression of human will – an idea that is captured in the concept of commander's intent[1] as part of the philosophy of mission command.[2] As such, the commander's entire effort (as well as that of his staff and subordinates), whether in planning, directing, allocating resources, supervising, motivating, and/or leading – is driven and governed by the commander's vision, goal, or mission and the will to realize or attain that vision, goal, or mission. In sum, command is the purposeful exercise of authority over structures, resources, people and activities.

But command is not a uni-dimensional concept. In many ways. it is similar to a tool belt that contains a number of implements that are designed to achieve specific results. It in fact rests on three pillars – authority, management and leadership. Each pillar is an integral and often inter-related component of command. Each can achieve a distinct effect. None are necessarily mutually exclusive – and when used judicially in accordance with prevailing circumstances and situational factors, combine to provide maximum effectiveness and success.

The first pillar is authority. Commanders can always rely on their authority to implement their will. Authority, which encompasses a legal and constitutional component (e.g. *National Defence Act*), is always derived from a higher or superior entity. It gives a commander the right to make decisions, transmit their intentions to subordinates and impose their will on others. It is military authority, namely by virtue of a service person's unlimited liability and the commander's vested authority to send individuals into harm's way, complete with the support of substantial penalties for non-conformance, that differentiates military command from civilian positions/appointments of power. Although authority is a powerful tool for commanders – reliance on rank and position will never build a cohesive, effective unit that will withstand the test of crisis. At best, it may present a chimera of an efficient organization, but even this is doubtful.

Notwithstanding that, at times, such as in crisis and/or in the face of individual or group intransigence to necessary change, it can provide the bludgeon required to clear the path to renewal or survival. The reliance on decisions, or actions by consensus at all times is an effective means of miring an organization into torpor. In some circumstances and occasions, authority must be the tool of choice.

The second pillar is management. Management is designed to control complexity and increase group effectiveness and efficiency. It is primarily concerned with the allocation and control of resources (i.e. human, financial and material) to achieve objectives. Its focus is staff action such as planning, organizing, staffing, directing and controlling. Management is also based on formal organizational authority and it is unequivocally results orientated. Its emphasis is on the correct and efficient execution of organizational processes. However, this is not to say that effective managers do not use leadership to increase their effectiveness in accomplishing their goals.

Clearly, management is of great importance to commanders and institutional leaders. Management skills and practices allow them to ensure that subordinates receive the necessary direction, guidance and resources – on time and where required – to achieve the mission in accordance with the commander's intent. As such, management is a critical and necessary component of command (and institutional leadership). However, it is not leadership, but then, neither should it be. It serves a distinct and vital purpose necessary to CF effectiveness and success. It neither replaces, nor substitutes for leadership. Rather, it is complimentary. It is but one of three instruments, designed to perform a specific function, in the command "tool belt."

The third pillar is leadership. It is the "human" side of command but it can also be exercised outside of the concept of command. It deals with the purpose of the organization – "doing the right thing" versus "doing it right [management]." In accordance with CF doctrine it is defined as "directing, motivating and enabling others to accomplish the mission professionally and ethically, while developing or improving capabilities that contribute to mission success." Whereas management is based on authority and position, leadership relies on influence, either direct or indirect.

In the end, the leadership component of command is about influencing people to achieve some objective that is important to the leader, the group, and the organization. It is the human element – leading, motivating, and inspiring, particularly during times of crisis, chaos and complexity when directives, policy statements and communiqués have little effect on cold, exhausted, and stressed subordinates. It is the very individualistic, yet powerful component that allows commanders and leaders at all levels to shape and/or alter the environment or system in which people function, and thereby influence attitudes, behaviour and the actions of others.

It is within this powerful realm of influence and potential change that leadership best demonstrates the fundamental difference between it and the concept of command. Too often, the terms command and leadership are interchanged or seen as synonymous. But, they are not. Leadership can, and should, be a component of command. After all, to be an effective commander, the formal authority that comes with rank and position must be reinforced and supplemented with personal qualities and skills – the human side. Nonetheless, as discussed earlier, command is based on vested authority and assigned position and/or rank. It may only be exercised downward in the chain of command through the structures and processes of control. Conversely, leadership is not constrained by the limits of formal authority. Individuals anywhere in the chain of command may, given the ability and motivation, influence peers and even superiors. This clearly differentiates leadership from command. In sum, although leadership is an essential role requirement for successful commanders, it is neither command, nor management.

Differentiating leadership from command and management is important in the context of institutional leadership because it is a critical component of creating lasting, enduring change. As noted earlier, although authority and management, as functions of command, provide the necessary capabilities to direct and guide the organization to effective achievement of its mandate, they rarely provide the necessary mechanism to ensure long term commitment from subordinates in the face of disconcerting, risk laden, ambiguous change.

As such, leadership, particularly transformational leadership, becomes the key component. It refers to a pattern of leader influence intended to alter the characteristics of individuals, organizations, or societies in a substantial way so that they are somehow more complete, or else better equipped to deal with the challenges they face or are likely to face. Clearly, transformational leadership has a particularly powerful and dynamic effect – it empowers people to take the necessary actions and decisions to achieve individual and institutional goals. In turn, this empowerment results in increased self-esteem and confidence, as well as self-actualization. In sum, this assists individuals in achieving more than they thought possible, which subsequently increases the overall organizational efficacy.

Transformational leadership is also key because it allows leaders to become active agents for change. Although not all change is necessarily good – and institutional leaders must be cautious not to be deluded into automatically equating any or all change with progress – necessary change can be best undertaken by empowering followers and providing them with voice. Transformational leadership allows institutional leaders to take the initiative in mobilizing people for participation in the processes of change, which in turn creates a sense of collective identity and purpose and once again increases the collective efficacy of an organization.

In the end, institutional leadership is about exactly that – creating the institutional and environmental conditions necessary for operational success. This entails shaping the environment by influencing subordinates through a clear mission and vision, as well as the provision of the necessary resources and policy, and the system and organizational structures to allow them to achieve success. It also means responding to their aspirations and legitimate needs, as well as providing a sense of identity, belonging and meaningfulness to their lives. This is not always easy, particularly for institutional leaders who must rely on indirect influence. However, the judicious application of authority, management and particularly leadership provide the necessary instruments to navigate the complex and ever changing environment that institutional leaders find themselves in.

SELECT BIBLIOGRAPHY

Bass, Bernard. *Transformational Leadership – Industrial, Military and Educational Impact.* Mahwah, NJ: LEA Publishers, 1998.

Bennis, Warren, Gretchen Spreitzer and Thomas Cummings, eds. *The Future of Leadership.* San Francisco: Jossey-Bass Publishers, 2001.

Burns, James MacGregor. *Transforming Leadership.* New York: Grove Press, 2003.

Canada. *Leadership in the Canadian Forces: Conceptual Foundations.* Kingston: DND, 2005.

Department of Defence. *Strategic Leadership Primer.* Carlisle, PA: US Army War College, 1998.

Harari, Oren. *The Leadership Secrets of Colin Powell.* New York: McGraw Hill, 2002.

Hughes, Richard L. and Katherine Colarelli Beatty. *Becoming a Strategic Leader.* San Francisco: Jossey-Bass, 2005.

Jaques, Elliott, and Stephen D. Clement. *Executive Leadership. A Practical Guide to Managing Complexity.* Arlington, VA: Blackwell Publishers, 1994.

Kets de Vries, Manfred. *The Leadership Mystique.* New York: Prentice Hall, 2001.

Koehler, Jerry W. and Joseph M. Pankowski. *Transformational Leadership in Government.* Delray Beach: St. Lucie Press, 1997.

Manske, Fred A. *Secrets of Effective Leadership.* Columbia: Leadership Education Development Inc., 1987.

Mintzberg, Henry, Bruce Ahlstrand, and Joseph Lampel. *Strategy Safari.* New York: The Free Press, 1998.

Nanus, Burt. *Visionary Leadership.* San Francisco: Jossey-Bass Publishers, 1992.

Perkins, Dennis N.T. *Leading at the Edge.* New York: Amacon, 2000.

Rost, Joseph C. *Leadership in the Twenty First Century.* Westport: Praeger, 1993.

Sullivan, Gordon R. and Michael V. Harper. *Hope is not a Method.* New York: Random House, 1996.

ENDNOTES

1   The Commander's intent is the commander's personal expression of why an operation is being conducted and what he hopes to achieve. It is a clear and concise statement of the desired end-state and acceptable risk. Its strength is the fact that it allows subordinates to exercise initiative in the absence of orders, or when unexpected opportunities arise, or when the original concept of operations no longer applies.

2   Mission Command is a command philosophy that promotes decentralized decision-making, freedom and speed of action and initiative. It entails three enduring tenets: the importance of understanding a superior commander's intent, a clear responsibility to fulfil that intent, and timely decision-making.

CHAPTER SIX

INSTITUTIONAL LEADER ETHICS

Dr. Daniel Lagacé-Roy

This article addresses the question of ethics as an important leader trait at the institutional level. The hallmark of ethics is to clarify concepts like "right" and "wrong" and how someone ought to live. This initial understanding of the meaning of ethics leads to its practicality and to the subject of leadership as a comprehensive example of how ethics influence the way that leaders lead. In other words, this article deals with *leadership ethics* as it refers to the understanding of ethical behaviour and climate (environment) applied to leadership. Emphasized by Joanne G. Ciulla, in her book, *Ethics, the Heart of Leadership*, ethics is at the heart of leadership. In the same vein, we argue that ethics is not only essential for leaders but, in fact, defines leadership.

Leaders, at the institutional level, are required to embrace strong ethical values and to be exemplars of ethical behaviour by establishing and emphasizing the ethical climate that is necessary to influence ethical behaviours. This ethical climate can be defined in general terms as norms, standards, expectations, perceptions, and practices accepted and reinforced by the leaders. One may ask: how does someone become an exemplar of good practices, for example? This question underlines our discussion throughout this article. In trying to answer it, two major points are highlighted: military ethos and leader development.

This article is divided in four parts. The first part looks at the 1990s, the period when leaders at the institutional level were challenged in their leadership. They were forced, as a consequence, to address not only the ethical aspect of their leadership, but also what defines the spirit of their profession, which is the military ethos. In the second part, we see that leaders recognized and understood that ethical behaviour and military ethos could not be separated. Furthermore, leaders are required, as exemplars of ethical behaviour, to adhere to and, more importantly, to internalize the military ethos that is embedded in Canadian values. The discussions regarding the definition of the military ethos led to the creation of the Defence Ethics Program (DEP) and to a formal definition in *Duty with Honour: The Profession of Arms in Canada*.

The third part demonstrates that ethical behaviour demands a personal identity development that is at the highest level. According to Robert Kegan, in his book *The Evolving Self: Problem and Process and Human Development*, the identity structure is exemplified at the institutional level by an understanding of how leaders see themselves and how they *make sense* of the organization they serve.[1] This making-sense, as we will see, has a direct impact on the way leaders lead.

The fourth part concludes with challenges for institutional leaders. These challenges serve as good examples of reinforcing the importance of embracing the military ethos as a living spirit. These challenges also emphasize that leader identity development is part of a continuum that encompasses an important shift from a manner of doing to a manner of being.

LOOKING BACK

In his article, "Canada: Managing Change with Shrinking Resources", Franklin Pinch wrote that the 1990s was a period when the Canadian Forces saw changes in the geopolitical scene, new kinds of peace operations, reductions in force strength, resource reductions, increased operational tempo, and new mission requirements.[2] Furthermore, according to Brian McKee in his research on *Canadian Demographic and Social Trends*, the CF realized that social changes were affecting the Defense organization: specifically, the declining birthrate in Canada, increasing multi-cultural diversity, and technological advances.[3] At the senior level within the organization, there were concerns about expectations for accountability, openness, and transparency. Trust, confidence, and responsibility were questioned and made public by publications like *Tarnished Brass: Crime and Corruption in the Canadian Military* by Scott Taylor and by *Une armée en déroute* by Michel Purnelle. Those changes and concerns were indications of an organization that needed to reflect upon its *raison d'être*.

During that period, events like the *Maclean's* magazine's sexual assault investigations, the Croatia contaminated soil allegations, and the Somalia incident reinforced criticism of the military leadership and tarnished the image of the Canadian Forces. The Somalia incident (1993) was, in fact, the turning point of that so-called "dysfunctional period" or "period of turmoil", expressions used in the *Debrief the Leaders* Project. In his book mentioned above, Taylor indicated that antisocial norms, beliefs, values and practices suggested a gap between professional and institutional loyalties, poor or inappropriate leadership, and lack of ethical conduct by senior leaders, all of which characterized that period of failures.

The erosion of an ethical environment led to a conclusion by the *Commission of Inquiry into the Deployment of Canadian Forces to Somalia* that the Somalia affair was attributable to a failure of military values. The values and beliefs studied by the Commission addressed the relationship between military and Canadian values, with particular attention given to professional values and the military ethos. In his early discussion of leadership in the CF in "Looking Back: Canadian Forces Leadership Problems and Challenges", as identified in recent military reports and generic studies, Karol Wenek emphasized that aspect.[4] In attributing the Somalia incident to a failure of military values, the Commission recognized the necessity to define the military ethos and its traditional core values, strengthening respect for the rule of law, and integrating Canadian societal values. These three core aspects, pertaining to the military, would also serve as driving forces in promulgating leader development. It was later suggested by other documents, e.g., *Officership in the 21st Century* and *The NCM Corps 2020*, that a new direction for officer and non-commissioned member (NCM) development should be clearly defined.

Moreover, training programs, professional activities, and education and performance assessments should be based on values and beliefs of the CF and Canadian society.

This brief account of the 1990s period reveals that the lack of leadership ethics by senior leaders damaged the image of the Canadian Forces. As a result, defining the military ethos for the 21st century became an imperative. In addition, leader development was recognized as an important condition in ensuring a constant adaptation to a changing world. It is clear that these two aspects (military ethos and leader development) were part of the same equation that defined the nature of ethics in the Canadian Forces.

MILITARY ETHOS

The severe scrutiny following the Somalia incident reinforced the need, in 1994, to articulate a military ethos.[5] This task had been previously undertaken in 1981 by General Ramsey Withers (then CDS). The 1981 Ethos statement was based on a specific ethical consideration: service before self. The focus of the 1994 Ethos statement, which was built on the first attempt, tried to bridge moral military virtues with values taken from the Canadian society. The 1994 statement failed to achieve consensus amongst the three different environments. Following that failure, a new agency called the Defence Ethics Program (DEP) was created within the Chief of Review Services Branch of the Vice Chief of the Defence Staff Group in order to pursue the work in place. A first draft of *Statement of Defence Ethics* was presented in July 1996. Instead of providing a statement of military ethos, the DEP concentrated its work on ethical obligations and principles for guiding ethical conduct. This statement was also designed for both military members and civilian employees of the Department of National Defence.

The DEP is a value-based program built on values that are fundamental to a democratic society. That value-based approach and the role of values were reflected in the Canadian military ethos described in *Duty with Honour: The Profession of Arms in Canada*. This publication defines the military ethos as "a living spirit – one that finds full expression through the conduct of members of the profession of arms."[6] Through this definition, *Duty with Honour* made it clear that military ethos requires more than simple adherence to a statement – or reliance on external codes of conduct – but demands a commitment to a profession characterized by its own sense of identity. This aspect of identity distinguishes members of Canadian Forces from the rest of the society and serves to develop the members' professional self-portrait.

Furthermore, *Duty with Honour* challenges military leaders to internalize the values, beliefs, and expectations that underpin the military ethos. In a different way, this challenge is expressed by Karol Wenek in his paper, "Wanted: A Military Ethos for the Postmodern Era", where he argues that beliefs, values, and attitudes have to "catch up" to institutional behaviour.[7] The full meaning of this challenge is that leaders, through the internalization of values, ought to be provided with the ethical framework for self-regulation. This self-regulation represents the obligation to independently regulate one's own actions and behaviours. More importantly, this self-regulation meets what the contemporary philosophy Michel Foucault, in an interview called "The ethics of the concern of the self as a practice of freedom," said about the sense in which the Greeks understood *ethos*: "a way of being and of behaviour."[8] Additionally, for those with leadership responsibilities, they have to develop and instill the capacity of self-regulation in others. However, this challenge cannot be achieved without a high level of identity development.

LEADER (IDENTITY) DEVELOPMENT

The introduction of this article advances that leaders at the institutional level should be the ones who establish and emphasize an ethical climate, while being exemplars of ethical behaviour. The expression of that behaviour encompasses values, beliefs, and expectations that are at the core of the military ethos. *Duty with Honour* and *Leadership in the Canadian Forces: Conceptual Foundations* have stressed the importance of a value-based approach to conduct and leadership. Furthermore, the Defence Ethics Program has entertained the notion that values influence the way military members, especially at the institutional level, should see themselves as professionals. However, that value-based approach implies that leaders have reached a certain level of understanding of *what* is an ethical climate and *how* ethical behaviours are a reflection of that climate. That approach conditioned them to a professional identity that directly influences how they conduct themselves.

In that context, the following questions should be asked: *how* do leaders construct their sense of identity as ethical institutional leaders? *How* do they see their role as members of the profession of arms? *How* do they lead the profession? *How* do they establish the necessary conditions for an environment that convey ethical conduct? The *how* is the center of gravity that sustains the fundamental process towards a more complex way of *making sense* of what is required by the military profession and the society. In other words, the fundamental question is: *how* do institutional leaders *make sense* of themselves as leaders?

According to Robert Kegan, the author mentioned in the introduction, this capacity of making sense (meaning-making) is associated with the structure of someone's identity development.[9] He argues that people evolve from a less complex to a more complex way of seeing themselves and the world. The term complex is defined as a change in "meaning-making," where internal and external experiences become more integrated in articulating a broader world view. This evolutionary process doesn't happen in a vacuum. It implies a change in a way of thinking and requires, as an example, the ability to analyze multiple aspects of a particular situation objectively. To a certain extent, this complex way of thinking means a deeper reflection of what is required when a particular situation is perceived. For the purpose of this paper, the question is to know which level of identity development is required for institutional leaders. At which level, for example, would a leader be able to influence the ethical conduct of followers? In other words, could identity development help leaders understand what constitutes ethical behaviour and what is required to foster an ethical climate?

Robert Kegan has identified 5 stages for explaining this evolutionary process. It is important, before exploring these stages further, to indicate that authors like Guindon, Aronson, and Cook, when writing about identity and moral development, usually make reference to Lawrence Kohlberg's work on moral development. Kegan does acknowledge Kohlberg's work by recognizing his contribution regarding the development of the personal construction of the social world (seen as an object) by a person (seen as a subject). In that personal construction, the subject and the object are *vis-à-vis*. In contrast, Kegan argues that the relationship between a subject and an object are not perceived as *vis-à-vis*, but invested in the same movement when trying to make sense of the social world. The features of Kegan's stages focus on the aspect of oneself that evolves towards an understanding of the systems and groups that shaped the person and of which the self is part. In order to illustrate and articulate the focus of these stages, the Defence Ethics program will serve as an example.

At **Stage 1**, only one perspective is perceived. The perception is single because the focus is only one aspect (one principle or one obligation) of the statement of ethics program. That perspective is seen as the only possibility to resolve a particular ethical dilemma. The DEP can also be considered the only ethical framework for all ethical situations. At that stage, there is no attempt to go beyond the structure of the program. At **Stage 2**, the awareness of more than one perspective is present, but the person will only deal with one perspective at the time. There is recognition that the DEP's ethical framework encompasses principles and obligations; however, the person will continue to deal with them separately. At that stage, there is an opening to what might constitute a larger picture of the program. These two first stages are considered for junior leaders, where the Ethics program serves as a guideline to be respected and followed. At **Stage 3**, there is an opening to reciprocal perspectives. To a certain extent, the person begins to negotiate with different aspects of the program (conflicting obligations and principles). That negotiation still involves self-interest (oneself), but there is an attempt to reach to alternative perspectives for solutions (how to resolve the conflict between two loyalties?) and the desire to internalize obligations and principles. Intermediate leaders are recognized at that stage. It is the lowest stage for senior leaders.

At **Stage 4**, the different perspectives and aspects of the program are not only external to the person but also internal in a way that a self-reflection of one's principles, obligations, and personal values are present when dealing with an ethical dilemma. That self-reflection implies the capacity to share and be critical of ideals. At that stage, a person has internalized principles and obligations, and his own sense of what constitutes an ethical dilemma. Furthermore, leaders at that level are less concerned with norms, rules, or regulations, but are engaged in reflections and discussions that influence these norms and rules. At **Stage 5**, the person recognizes a plurality of systems, groups and organizations that are interrelated and are seen as "universal." The DEP is not viewed as an entity unto itself, but it is an element of a larger framework or system that defines a group or an organization. The program is designed to help CF members and DND employees make the right decisions when ethical dilemmas occurred. However, for senior leaders, the program is not only a tool or a guide for resolving particular situations, but it also serves as a mechanism for fostering a more ethical climate in the CF. As such, senior leaders will ask themselves if the program does serve that purpose.

Kegan's model describes leaders, as they evolve from one stage to the next, as developing a personal identity that corroborates with the construct of a broader view of the organization, the society, and the world. This model emphasizes that leaders – at higher stages – recognize their own perspective process when dealing with complex issues. In that sense, that perspective process is a desired outcome of the values-based leadership. When concerned with the well-being of their members, for example, leaders should provide a sound approach on *how* a program (such as the DEP) or a policy (such as gender integration) will best serve the interests of the CF members in different situations and settings. This approach will have an indirect influence on the people and the institution. When leaders analyze, inspire, contribute, and implement changes that are valued by the institution at large,[10] they perform "transformational leadership" that is considered ethical, since they influence followers' basic attitudes, beliefs and values by empowering them with the feeling of self-regulation and self-commitment. Therefore, their indirect contribution has a direct influence on the understanding of ethical behaviour and ethical climate. Their leadership, according to Edward Aronson in his research "Integrating Leadership Styles and Ethical Perspectives," exemplifies the follower's internal sense of responsibility and expectation to do what is right.

CHALLENGES AND CONCLUSIONS

"The higher the position, the more complex and less precise are the [ethical] issues." This quote from Clay T. Buckingham in his article "Ethics and the Senior Officer: Institutional Tensions",[11] captures the essential of how ethics, at the senior level, are critical. In 2001, Major-General K.G. Penney made a similar observation in "A Matter of Trust: Ethics and Self-Regulation among Canadian Generals," by affirming that ethical behaviour is a fundamental requirement for senior positions where the expectation of accountability is greatest.[12] Penney was echoing not only his own perception of what is required of senior officers, but different point of views from other general officers (called "The group of fourteen") who first met in 1998 at RMC to discuss ethical dimensions for generalship. It was clear, from those meetings, that generals were concerned about gray zones. Conflict of ethical obligations was at the forefront, as they reviewed concepts like loyalty up versus loyalty down, responsibility versus privilege, and transparency versus political correctness. For Penney, it was the duty of senior officers to lead by example, to open the dialogue on ethical issues and to foster innovation, initiative, and trust. They are responsible for creating a climate in which unethical behaviour, "no matter how subtle, no matter how private," is unacceptable because it erodes morale and contradicts the military ethos.

Such discourse is very encouraging; however, how does the CF prepare officers at the institutional level for these "gray zones?" How can the CF prepare its senior personnel to perform in dangerous and complex environments in which they will encounter contradictory societal and institutional expectations regarding the well-being of the military members?

Answering that question is not an easy task. We can address it by focusing on an introspective view of what is needed at that level. This article already mentioned the necessity for a high level of identity development. Our discussion goes further by insisting that this level of development is absolutely required, along with knowledge and interpersonal skills, qualities mentioned by Brigadier-General K.C. Hague in "Strategic Thinking General/Flag Officers: The Role of Education."[13] Those qualities or attributes are, according to William Glover in " 'We reposing especial trust and confidence in your loyalty, courage, and integrity', The Officer Corps of 2020", the product of an open mind and more especially an educated mind.[14] The meaning of an educated mind refers to the ability to adapt rapidly and to be flexible while demonstrating initiative. The value of education is paramount and is considered as an intrinsic value when it comes to developing and mastering knowledge and critical thinking. In addition to education, senior leaders could increase their awareness by sharing experiences and concerns. This dialogue between leaders could result in a certain type of informal mentorship and might enhance the understanding of the notion that leaders have to be seen as exemplars of ethical behaviour.

In conclusion, leaders at the institutional level are challenged in the way they lead. Leading by personal example is a value in itself, however it becomes a cliché when leaders don't grasp the concept of self-awareness and self-regulation. The challenge of the self is a matter of considerable personal maturity and ethics. Senior leaders are in a unique position to embody ethics as a force multiplier. They have the legitimate authority to create an ethical climate within a more transformational leadership approach, with which

CF members could identify themselves and buy-in with their espoused vision. In that ethical climate, CF members are not means but ends to achieve mission success. This sense of duty or obligation towards CF members is the foundation upon which leaders build their ethical climate. In that context, members of all ranks will do what is right and will go beyond their own self-interests for the good of the institution.

SELECT BIBLIOGRAPHY

Aronson, Edward. "Integrating Leadership Styles and Ethical Perspectives," *Canadian Journal of Administrative Sciences/Revue canadienne des sciences de l'administration*. Vol 18, No. 4, December 2001.

Buckingham, Clay T. "Ethics and the Senior Officer: Institutional tensions", *Parameters*, Vol 25, No. 2, Summer 1995.

Brown, Michael. E., Linda K. Trevino and David A. Harrison. "Ethical leadership: A social learning perspective for construct development and testing". *Organizational Behavior and Human Decision Processes*. Vol. 97, No. 2, July 2005.

Ciulla, Joanna B, ed. *Ethics, the Heart of Leadership*. Westport, CT: Quorum Books, 1998.

Cook, Martin L. *The Moral Warrior.* New York: State University of New York Press, 2004.

Forsythe, G.B., S. Snook, P. Lewis and P. Bartone. "Making Sense of Officership: Developing a Professional Identity for 21st Century Army Officers," in, L.J. Matthew, ed. *The Future of the Army Profession*. New York: McGraw-Hill Primis Custom Publishing, 2002.

Glover, William. "We reposing especial trust and confidence in your loyalty, courage, and integrity," in B. Horn, ed. *Contemporary issues in officership*: *A Canadian perspective*. Toronto, ON: Canadian Institute of Strategic Studies, 2000.

Guindon, André. *Le développement moral*. Ottawa: Novalis, 1989.

Kanungo, Rabindra N. "Ethical Values of Transactional and Transformational Leaders," *Canadian Journal of Administrative Sciences/Revue canadienne des sciences de l'administration,* Vol 18, No. 4, December 2001.

Kanungo, Rabindra N. and Manuel Mendonca. *Ethical Dimensions of Leadership.* Thousand Oaks, CA: SAGE Publications, 1996.

Kegan, Robert. *The Evolving Self: Problem and Process in Human Development.* Cambridge: Harvard University Press, 1982.

Lang, Anthony F. Jr., Albert C. Pierce and Joel H. Rosenthal, eds. *Ethics and the Future of Conflict.* New Jersey: Pearson Prentice Hall, 2004.

Maak, Thomas and Nicola M. Pless. *Responsible Leadership.* London, New York: Routledge, 2006.

ENDNOTES

1   Robert Kegan, *The evolving self: problem and process in human development* (Cambridge: Harvard University Press, 1982), 103.

2   Franklin C. Pinch, "Canada: Managing Change with Shrinking Resources" in Charles C. Moskos, John Allen Williams and David R. Segal, eds., *The Postmodern Military: Armed Forces after the Cold War* (New York: Oxford University Press, 2000), 161.

3   Brian McKee, *Canadian Demographic and Social Trends* (DND: Directorate of Strategic Human Resources, November, 2002) 2.

4   Karol Wenek, "Looking Back: Canadian Forces Leadership Problems and Challenges identified in recent reports and studies" (Unpublished document, June 2002), 8.

5   This section is based on Pierre Lépine's Doctoral thesis: "Blurred vision: Ethos and the Canadian Forces" (Calgary: Center for Military and Strategic Studies, 2002).

6   *Duty with Honour: The Profession of Arms in Canada* (Kingston: Canadian Forces Leadership Institute, 2003) 34.

7   Karol, Wenek, "Wanted: A Military Ethos for the Postmodern Era", Paper presented at the Conference on Leadership in the Armies of Tomorrow and the Future (Kingston, 6–7 February, 2002) 27.

8   Michel Foucault, "The ethics of the concern of the self as a practice of freedom" in Paul Rabinow, ed., *Michel Foucault:*

Ethics, Subjectivity and Truth, Volume 1 (New York: The New Press, 1997) 286.

9   For a study using Kegan's framework, see G.B. Forsythe, S. Snook, P. Lewis and P. Bartone, " Making sense of Officership: developing a professional identity for 21st century army officers" in L. J. Matthew, ed., *The Future of the Army Profession,* (New York: McGraw-Hill Primis Custom Publishing, 2002) 357-378.

10   The aspect of "change" is emphasized in Chapter 5 of this book. In his chapter "Institutional Leadership – Understanding the Command, Management and Leadership Nexus", Colonel Bernd Horn stated that "Transformational leadership is also key because it allows leaders to become active agents of change".

11   Clay T. Buckingham, "Ethics and the Senior Officer: Institutional tensions", *Parameters,* Vol 25, No. 2, (Summer 1995) 101.

12   K.G. Penney , "A Matter of Trust: Ethics and Self-Regulation among Canadian Generals" in B. Horn, ed., *Generalship and the Art of the Admiral,* (St. Catherines: Vanwell Publishing Limited, 2001) 156.

13   K.C. Hague, "Strategic Thinking General/Flag Officers: The Role of Education" in B. Horn, ed., *Generalship and the Art of the Admiral,* (St. Catherines: Vanwell Publishing Limited, 2001) 509.

14   William, Glover, " 'We reposing especial trust and confidence in your loyalty, courage, and integrity', The Officer Corps of 2020", in B. Horn, ed., *Contemporary Issues in Officership: A Canadian Perspective.* (Toronto, ON: Canadian Institute of Strategic Studies, 2000) 41.

CHAPTER SEVEN

CONFIGURING A PROFESSIONAL DEVELOPMENT FRAMEWORK TO ADDRESS CANADIAN FORCES LEADERSHIP CHALLENGES

Dr. Robert W. Walker

The changing nature of society, the global security environment, and technological innovation necessitate an aggressive Canadian Forces (CF) approach to understanding leadership, to ensuring leader effectiveness through a congruence of institutional demands and leader capabilities, and to providing continuous professional development (PD) for CF leaders. The CF, as a military organization with a profession of arms imbedded within it, and as an institution committed to mission success, needs to balance and to successfully address the integrated demands that evolve from its organizational facets and its professional responsibilities. Current and ongoing CF transformation initiatives magnify these demands, reflect the increasing challenges for military professionalism, and underscore the pronounced need for tenacity, decisiveness and versatility in CF leaders.

The examination of professionalism and the profession of arms, effective leadership requirements, institutional effectiveness, and requisite leader capabilities progressed through a substantial research effort using military, professional, and generic leadership literature, as well as direct guidance from military leaders and other subject matter experts. This research supported the production of the CF manuals that effectively and successfully articulate the situation and circumstances of the CF and the general requirements for leadership in the CF.

This chapter identifies the leadership research and military initiatives that supported the creation of a Professional Development Framework for leaders of the CF. Reviews previously were conducted to enumerate the CF's responsibilities for the early 21st century. Concurrently, the organizational literature was researched to articulate generic "effectiveness" at institutional levels. Subsequently, a context-specific model for CF Effectiveness was generated, incorporating the corporate outcomes and the conduct values to serve as the institutional backdrop against which leaders would function. The CF manuals, *Leadership in the Canadian Forces: Conceptual Foundations* (2005) and *Leadership in the Canadian Forces: Leading the Institution* provide an in-depth articulation of these steps necessary to define the CF as an institution and to describe the important circumstances for the CF to be institutionally effectiveness. Accordingly, this chapter provides only a general review of that effectiveness.

With CF Effectiveness defined, the subsequent focus became the means to ensure CF leadership and its application to challenges of war, global issues, security threats, internal order and member care. Leader characteristics, competencies, skills and knowledge, etc., were studied in order to generate frameworks of relevant leader capacities, including those needed for the CF. *Leadership in the Canadian Forces: Leading the Institution* described this process in which the result was a five-element cluster of requisite CF leader domains: **Expertise, Cognitive Capacities, Social Capacities, Change Capacities** and **Professional Ideology**.

This cluster of five requisite elements then was integrated with a continuum of four leader levels (junior, intermediate, advanced, senior) to generate a Professional Development Framework. This Framework constituted a template for defining the necessary leader knowledge and capacities and a military professionalism across the continuum of levels of leadership, as well as determining the most relevant subject matter and most effective learning strategies to develop these leader elements.

The consequence was a comprehension of the necessary *congruence* between the CF Effectiveness model – representing the institution – and the CF Professional Development Framework – representing the CF leadership. Such congruence is a prerequisite, but not a guarantee, for CF success in various missions, initiatives and other applications, a number of which are exemplified in this chapter. Figure 1 is a stylized flowchart depicting the pathways to congruence of institution and leadership.

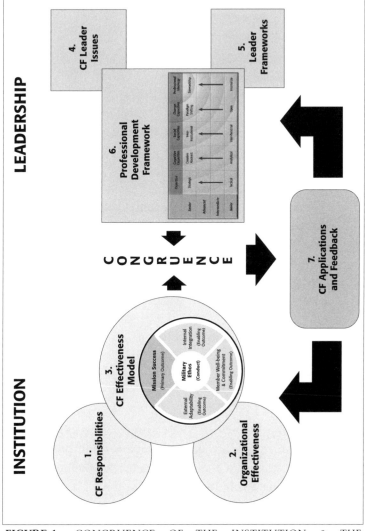

FIGURE 1. CONGRUENCE OF THE INSTITUTION & THE LEADERSHIP

The next seven sections of this chapter provide details about significant components contributing to a crucial institution – leadership congruence. Sections 1–3 briefly address the institution of the CF. Sections 4–6 address the leadership.

Section 7 addresses CF applications and outcomes resulting from effective congruence. The Sections address:

1. An enumeration of *Canadian Forces Responsibilities* in the 21st century.

2. An articulation of the literature on *Organizational Effectiveness.*

3. A generating of a context-specific *Canadian Forces Effectiveness* model as the institutional backdrop against which leaders function.

4. A defining of the means – CF leadership – to ensure CF effectiveness, and the *Canadian Forces Leader Issues* and challenges therein.

5. A creating of taxonomies and *Leader Frameworks* of generic leader capacities, including those needed for the CF, from a review of the literature. The result was the CF-specific, five-element cluster of requisite leader capacities.

6. An integration of the cluster of requisite elements with a continuum of four CF leader levels (junior, intermediate, advanced, senior) to construct a *Professional Development Framework* for the CF.

7. A presentation of successful *CF Applications*, such as CF Transformation, operational mission success, human resources systems review, and professional development of senior CF leaders evolving from the appropriate congruence between the CF Effectiveness model and the Professional Development Framework.

THE INSTITUTION – THE CANADIAN FORCES

Section 1: Canadian Forces Responsibilities

In order to work with the broader concepts of institution, leadership and institution-leadership congruence, it was necessary first to assemble a thorough representation of the responsibilities of the institution, i.e., to articulate the responsibilities for which the organization takes charge and can become institutionally effectiveness.

Prior to publication of the CF leadership manuals in 2005, Mr. Karol Wenek, an ex-CF officer and a subject matter expert on professionalism and leadership, wrote extensively on the CF, its responsibilities, and its leadership.[1] Other scholars, defence analysts and defence scientists also listed significant CF challenges for the 21st century such as Canada-US relations, emerging technology, force restructuring, and resourcing for military transformation, all in a global circumstance of new security threats, failing states, pandemic diseases, migration, religious extremism and narco-cartels.[2]

The CF responsibilities for its leaders related to the major functions of leading people and leading the institution along the effectiveness dimensions of mission success, internal integration, member well-being and commitment, external adaptability, and in line with military ethos. The *Leadership in the Canadian Forces: Conceptual Foundations* manual provides greater detail.[3] Leader responsibilities, of course, vary in accordance with different levels of leadership, e.g., the stratified systems theory of leadership, studied within US militaries and many large civilian organizations, identifies seven institutional levels for differentiating leadership responsibilities, roles and scopes of influence.[4]

Singularly important in the review and articulation of CF responsibilities was the research on the profession of arms in Canada (*Duty with Honour: The Profession of Arms* in Canada in book and booklet/*Summary* format). The profession of arms constitutes the essence, the milieu, the ambience in which CF leaders conduct their responsibilities.

In summary, these multiple-perspective reviews and approaches support and validate the diverse responsibilities of CF leaders. These leader responsibilities substantially guided the subsequent development of a CF Effectiveness model, a leader cluster of requisite elements and attributes, and a Professional Development Framework.

Section 2: Organizational Effectiveness

The next, important step in working through the components represented schematically in Figure 1 was the focus on organizational effectiveness. This involved the identification and review of existing (theory-based, empirically-derived, current government and CF) models and frameworks for organizational effectiveness.

Wenek's research, cited above, including the examination of a particularly strong and relevant organizational effectiveness model titled A Competing Values Framework and created by Robert Quinn.[5] In brief, Quinn's Competing Values Framework represents 30 different criteria of effectiveness in organizations, including such positive and negative variables as efficiency, quality, growth, attrition, motivation, control, information management, participation, productivity, accidents/safety, morale, conflict, cohesion, planning, satisfaction, and training/development.[6] The statistical reduction of this collection of variables yielded two major imperatives that were integrated into Quinn's effectiveness framework. Leaders, in order to generate institutional effectiveness, must comprehend the inherent but related contradictions in outcomes necessary for institutional effectiveness, and must be sufficiently flexible to balance the competing demands. Quinn stated, "It requires a dramatic change in outlook, a redefinition of one's world view. It means transcending the rules of mechanistic logic used for solving well-defined problems and adopting a more comprehensive and flexible kind of logic."[7]

Section 3: Canadian Forces Effectiveness

Quinn's Competing Values Framework was identified as having the greatest potential for the creation of a CF Effectiveness model. Applying it as an institutional effectiveness model to the CF, the major components for CF effectiveness were identified (Figure 2): Mission Success, Member Well-Being and Commitment, Internal Integration and External Adaptability. The complexity of leadership and the challenge to military leaders was evident in these competing outcomes and priorities – getting the primary mission

accomplished while maintaining the well-being and commitment of the members in the organization, generating and
maintaining internal order and cohesion, and adapting to and
shaping external change.

FIGURE 2. CANADIAN FORCES EFFECTIVENESS

However, there is a significant difference between a defence
organization and a professional military institution. An accurate CF Effectiveness model also needed to reflect that the
major outcomes are pursued in accordance with a definable
set of individual professional values (a professional ideology)
incorporated into an institutional military ethos. To do this,
the CF Effectiveness model incorporates a military ethos
with a pragmatic military moral value system, a vision of
duty with honour, and an informing vision of social utility to
Canada and its people.

In summary, the four outcomes constitute organizational
effectiveness, while the component of military ethos constitutes professional effectiveness. Integrating all five aspects, the
equation is:

Institutional/CF Effectiveness =
Organizational Effectiveness + Professional Effectiveness.

To this point, the focus has been the CF as an institution. This
chapter has addressed institutional and leader responsibilities,

aspects of organizational effectiveness, and the creation of the CF Effectiveness model. The focus now shifts to the other half of the important institution – leadership congruence: effectiveness in leaders, with its components being: CF leader issues; leader frameworks or taxonomies; the creation of the Professional Development Framework; and the successful CF applications following from that successful institution–leadership congruence.

THE LEADERSHIP – THE LEADERS

Section 4: Canadian Forces Leader Issues

The CF is experiencing perpetual transformation. Nothing is static. The predominant constant is change. The working circumstances of all members are in a state of flux. This complexity continues to increase in the roles and responsibilities of CF leaders. With this complexity comes the need for evolving leader proficiencies and enhanced leader attributes that can ensure flexibility in leader focus and leader styles whether leading people or leading the institution. The challenges to members from change seem endless:

Change at Global Levels. For the CF, the end of the Cold War, followed by the 1990's with its substantial and sequential CF budget cuts, created new and complex leadership challenges. Peacekeeping evolved into peacemaking, conflict resolution, and outright combat in regional pop-up wars. Terrorism, homeland security, and post-9/11 regional wars have followed as the foci of the 21st century. Current CF member warfighting in Afghanistan, with fatal outcomes, reflects the most recent and tragic complexities in leadership challenges.[8] The war between Israel and the Hezbollah in Lebanon does the same.

Leading People/Leading the Institution. Another challenge for leaders is the evolving emphasis and change, or foci, of leading people and leading the institution across the continuum of leader levels. Importantly, leading people and leading the institution are not dichotomous but in fact are two, always present, aspects of a leadership approach. The difference pertains to an increased emphasis on leading the institution as one acquires greater rank and responsibilities. The purpose and the general objectives are the same up and down the continuum, however the process evolves and the specifics of the requisite attributes change.

Leadership Focus. Another aspect of change is in "leadership focus". The majority of CF leaders are at levels of leadership where the leading of people is the predominant leadership activity, and that activity is mission oriented. Leadership that is military task-centred, direct and face-to-face, and more transactional than transformational, is most appropriate to influence followers in situations of operations, combat, and critical responsive action. For leading the institution, where more consultative, policy development-oriented, organizationally-flattened circumstances exist, a more effective leadership focus is one for influencing subordinates or colleagues in personal-(not position)-powered, knowledge-driven change-shaping, non-urgent situations.

Leadership Style. A profound factor for CF members experiencing the transition from junior to senior leader status, either as officers or as senior NCOs, is this necessary transition of leadership style. A leader commitment is needed to the evolution of a style away from people as followers in action-oriented situations to a leader style for members and others in non-hierarchical teams, collaborative groups, consultative committees and advisory units at peer or quasi-peer levels, groups that are committed to support of institutional initiatives and progress. The most senior leader, as "boss", no longer can be expected to have all of the answers or, possibly, even a sense of the best alternatives.

Change at Work-Site levels. At the micro end of the continuum of change stands the individual member with an individual job and set of duties. But, due to rapid change, for an individual leader, the boundaries of his/her job need to be far less precise and permanent than in the past century. Figure 3 reflects this transformation. The evolution in leader responsibilities partly is generated by the current shift in perspectives of the work/worker interface as postmodern society evolves from the modern era, from the industrial age to the information age. The "old" 20th century alignment between workers and their organizations, necessary to achieve institutional effectiveness, has been distorted by change and transition.

A CURRENT CONTEXT FOR CHANGE		
	Work-Oriented	Worker-Oriented
Era	Modern	Postmodern
Toffler Wave	Industrial	Information/ Knowledge
Theory	X, Domination	Y & Z, Reciprocal Relations
Icon	Henry Ford, Fred Taylor	Bill Gates, Steve Jobs
Org Chart	Hierarchy, Bureaucracy	Matrix, Networks, Pods
Stereotype	Brawn: Assembly Line	Brains: Hi-Tech, Degrees
Job Location	Steel Plant, Factory	Software Design Offices
Job Framework	Org Chart/ Job Description	Goals, Projects, Change
Job Info/Detail	Tasks, Time x Percentages	Knowledge, Attributes
Process/Detail	Occupational/ Job Analysis	Competencies, Skills
Leader Power	Positional, Role/Rank	Personal, Exemplar
Leadership	More Transactional	More Transformational
Military Profession	Warrior + Technician	Warrior + Technician + Scholar + Diplomat

FIGURE 3.   THE WORK FOCUS / THE WORKER FOCUS

This current transformation in job-person fit from a work-orientation to a worker-orientation is one more challenge to current leaders. Responsibilities in an increasing proportion of jobs and positions are no longer only those circumscribed by the organizational chart boxes and job descriptions, but are determined as much by an individual worker's/leader's *full backpack* of capacities, expertise, characteristics, attributes and potential. Work definitions are hybrids of the job/task responsibilities cross-pollinated with the member's leader characteristics and attributes with only generally specified worker responsibilities.

To summarize, the institution of national defence in western societies is changing rapidly. Philosophies, concepts, principles and technologies are in a state of change. Importantly, the systematic elevation of CF leaders through promotion to senior leader levels adds additional requirements for leadership change and leader competency transformation. Change creates ambiguities in leadership doctrine and leadership definitions such that the cluster of requisite leader competencies, the "right stuff", needs to capture and contain these ambiguities.

Section 5: Leader Frameworks

Some Background. To determine and to inclusively define the effective CF requisite leader elements and attributes, a valid and legitimate process for creating taxonomies or frameworks was needed. A consortium of industrial/organizational psychologists from or affiliated with St. Mary's University, Dr. Shaun Newsome, Dr. Arla Day, and others, generated a sound and useful procedure for creating context- or organization-specific leader competency frameworks.[9] They researched the processes of leader assessment, evaluation and development, and then they identified procedural steps for identifying leader competencies. These steps included reviewing existing and context-specific information, consulting with key stakeholders, soliciting subject matter experts, validating draft competencies, and finalizing frameworks of the leader competencies.

Processes outlined by Newsome and colleagues had implications for the identification of a cluster of CF requisite leader elements that could generate institutional effectiveness. Relevant generic and military literatures on institutional effectiveness exist, covering taxonomies for leader attributes, their definitions, proficiency levels, etc. An early, simple, generic, industrial-era, three-sector taxonomy of work skills consisted of technical skills, thinking skills and interpersonal skills.[10] More recently, in 2001, renowned American organizational guru Dr. Stephen Zaccaro, after extensive, applied, research on military and non-military leadership, created a complete five-cluster taxonomy of characteristics or components that he labeled Expertise and Knowledge, Cognitive Capacities and Skills, Social Capacities and Skills, Personality, and Motivation.[11]

Zaccaro's consolidation of leader domains generated from numerous findings from independent researchers and other subject matter experts, plus related research and articles, was a breakthrough, the importance of which, depicted in Table 1, cannot be understated. His taxonomy of only five domains covers the functional expertise and knowledge required; the "intelligence" and creative and reasoning capacities; the "people skills" of communicating, negotiating, influencing and understanding; the preference to grow and achieve and improve and change, and to influence others to do likewise; and the character dispositions of openness to ideas and experiences, to exercise initiative and confidence and assertiveness, and to be trustful and courageous and stable.

Karol Wenek[12] generated Table 1 by utilizing Zaccaro's military-based, five-component taxonomy as an anchoring framework to display five other researchers'[13] approximate equivalents to Zaccaro's leadership taxonomy. An appropriate, context-specific, leader framework for an organization such as the CF would need to be structured as a collection of the relevant leader elements or capacities, characteristics, knowledge and expertise of its effective leaders. The CF need for such a structured framework was complicated and could involve:

- generating, at a macro level, a leader framework of institution-wide, unique but interconnected, leader elements that together would constitute a leader framework.;

- at the next level, each of these elements/capacities would encapsulate a set of leader attributes that also would have institution-wide application;

- at the third, micro, level, specific competencies applicable to different sets or sub-sets of leaders in specific positions, ranks or assignments would be defined and developed. Below this micro level, sub-levels with specific sub-competencies applicable to different sub-sets of leaders also could be defined and developed; and

- a dictionary of definitions, a continuum with descriptions of proficiency levels for each competency, plus activities or behaviourally anchored indicators for each proficiency level, would supplement such a multi-layered framework.

A crucial factor here is that institutional effectiveness for the CF can be achieved only through application of the capacities of *military* leaders. The important construct that is needed, then, is a *context-specific* CF leader framework of elements and attributes that, when implemented within an effective institution, will support military applications with maximum expectations of success.

Toward the CF Context-Specific Framework. CFLI researchers Alan Okros, Karol Wenek and the author conceptualized a draft macro-to-micro CF leader hierarchy of leader capacities.[14] It was determined, however, that for creating a CF leader taxonomy and context-specific leader structure reflective of the rapidly changing times and militarily unique professional practices, recently published research and generic literature were inadequate. The literature had not kept up with evolving leadership challenges. As examples of the shortcomings in the literature, aspects of the research preceded much of this current, explosive information era, the "learning organization" phenomena, and leadership of emphatic change on a hostile globe.

The earlier leadership research and resulting literature of the industrial era and the Cold War period that ended just over 15 years ago, had explored generic and military leadership mostly as position-based and interpersonal transactions with

TABLE 1. APPROXIMATE EQUIVALENCIES ACROSS LEADERSHIP/MANAGEMENT TAXONOMIES

See pages 136 & 137

Executive Characteristics (Zaccaro, 1996)	Public Service EX competencies (PSC, 1999)	Managerial skills & traits (Yukl, 1999)
Cognitive Capacities & Skills Intelligence Analytical reasoning skills Synthesis & mental modeling Metacognitive skills Verbal/writing skills Creativity	Cognitive capacity Creativity Visioning Action management Organizational awareness	Analytical ability Logical thinking Concept formation Judgement Problem-solving skills Creativity
Social Capacities & Skills Social reasoning skills Behavioural flexibility Negotiating/persuasions skills Conflict-management skills	Teamwork Partnering Interpersonal relations communication	Empathy Social sensitivity Understanding of behaviour Communications skills Persuasion skills
Personality Openneess Curiosity Self-discipline Flexibility Risk propensity Internal locus of control	Stamina/stress resistance Ethics and values Stable personality Behavioural flexibility	Openness to experience Integrity, character, courage Emotional maturity Confidence & composure Flexiblility & self-monitoring High energy & stress tolerance
Motivation Need for achievement Socialized power motive Self-efficacy	Self-confidence	Socialized power motive
Expertise & Knowledge Knowledge of environment Functional expertise Social expertise	Domain Knowledge	Technical proficiency

Leader Attributes (Gardner, 1990)	Leadership Competencies (Tett, et al., 2000)	Managerial Competencies (Spencer & Spencer, 1993)
Intelligence & judgement Planning & setting priorities	Problem awareness Short-term planning Strategic planning Creative thinking Monitoring	Analytical Thinking : sees implications of situations : analyzes issues systematically : anticipates obstacles Conceptual Thinking : sees non-obvious patterns : notices discrepancies : rapidly identifies key issues
Skills in dealing with people Understanding of followers Capacity to motivate	Motivating by authority Motivating by persuasion Team building Listening Oral communication Public presentation Developing self & others Tolerance Cultural appreciation Directing Decision delegation Co-ordinating Goal-setting	Impact & Influence : uses data or information : appeals to reason or logic : uses examples Teamwork & Co-operation : improves morale, resolves conflicts : involves others, solicits imput : gives credit or recognition Developing Others : gives constructive feedback : reassures after difficulties : coaches, suggests, explains : gives developmental assignments Interpersonal Understanding : knows others' attitudes & needs : reads non-verbal behaviour : understands motivation Team Leadership : communicates high standards : stands up for group, gets resources Relationship Building
Courage, resolution Trustworthiness Confidence Dominance, assertiveness Flexibility Physical vitality & stamina	Compassion Co-operation Sociability Politeness Political astuteness Assertiveness Seeking input Dependability Initiative Urgency Decisiveness	Initiative : seizes opportunities : handles crises swiftly : pushes envelope of authority : shows tenacity & persistence Self-confidence : confident in abilities & judgement : enjoys challenging tasks : questions/challenges superiors : accepts responsibility for failure Assertiveness : sets limits : sets standards, demands quality : confronts performance problems Information Seeking : gathering information systematically : curious, asks diagnostic questions
Need to achieve Willingness to accept responsibility	Task focus	Achievement Orientation : sets goals : measures progress & performance : improves efficiency/ effectiveness
Task competence	Occupational acumen Productivity	Organizational Awareness Technical Background

relatively static organizational backgrounds of situational variables - a reflection of Henry Ford's time rather than Bill Gates' era. Only recently has leadership been redefined for its transformational emphasis and impact on both people and institutions through a leadership of inspiration and change within a learning-organization setting. This project enhanced existing literature and research by addressing these factors.

Additionally, the generic "industrial" literature has not addressed the concept of professionalism nor dealt with profession-integrated or profession-dominated institutions such as articulated in *Duty with Honour: The Profession of Arms in Canada*. The Canadian military's profession of arms has its own unique characteristics of expertise, responsibility and identity, characteristics that demand specific and unique leader attributes not addressed in generic taxonomies and frameworks. The internalization of the military ethos, its beliefs, values and expectations, is fundamental to a military life and career with its unlimited liability and spirit of self-sacrifice and dedication to duty in life-threatening situations and theatres, without regard to personal fear or danger. That ethos includes a fighting spirit with the moral, physical and intellectual qualities to achieve success in military operations, an adherence to a personal and professional discipline to achieve objectives through unit cohesion and a high placement on teamwork that maximizes individual cooperation.

The challenge, therefore, was to develop an effective leader framework that would surpass all current frameworks as one that fully accommodated the evolving and increasingly effective leader practices needed in the CF, including the unique leader attributes of an internalized ethos and moral reasoning of a professional ideology, and learning/change capacities. Through modification and tailoring of Zaccaro's five element taxonomy (See Table 1) created from extensive research of military and non-military leadership, and with due consideration of a number of other leader-qualities taxonomies, a CF leader framework was created.

Wenek previously articulated how the classic taxonomy of technical, cognitive and interpersonal skills had evolved into a taxonomy of five categories – moral, technical, interpersonal, cognitive, and adaptable.[15] In more recent writings, Wenek grouped the elements into five general categories: knowledge and skills/expertise, cognitive abilities, social capacities, personality/adaptability, and motivation/values/professionalism.[16] Zaccaro's five categories and Wenek's five-class taxonomy have strong and justified similarities. The amalgamation of requisite CF leader capacities relied heavily on these consolidations by Zaccaro and by Wenek, as well as guidance from other sources.

The Requisite CF Leader Elements. Consolidation of the findings in the literature on requisite leader competencies, and on structuring taxonomies to best reflect the interdependent and interactive clusters of necessary leader attributes (Table 1), confirmed that effective leaders, as they acquire experience and advancement, especially require: strong cognitive/thinking capacities; flexible and articulate social/behavioural capacities; capacities to respond to and shape change in learning-organization settings; and technical expertise and institutional knowledge; all integrated with a professional ideology that supports a mastery of the profession of arms.

Therefore, by consolidating and incorporating this supportive leadership literature into a systematic and sequential categorization process that included the context-specific dynamics of a profession of arms institution, five leader elements were identified as collectively constituting a CF leader framework – *Expertise, Cognitive Capacities, Social Capacities, Change Capacities*, and *Professional Ideology.*

Brief descriptions of the leader elements and their attributes are provided at Table 2. A total of 16 attributes required of all CF leaders are nested within these five elements. Each attribute in turn would consist of a collated grouping of position-, level-, and role-specific competencies which are not yet identified. They would, however, be in line with human resources systems needs, i.e., performance assessment, succession planning, promotion, etc.

A FRAMEWORK OF 5 LEADER ELEMENTS	16 ATTRIBUTES (IN BOLD) WITHIN 5 ELEMENTS ACROSS THE LEADER CONTINUUM
	The focus, scope, magnitude of Competencies for responsibilities related to the leader attributes will vary with rank, leader level, position, etc., and usually increase with time in CF, rank, seniority and credibility.
EXPERTISE	Expertise consists of **Specialist** (Military Occupation Classification) **and Technical** (clusters, e.g., combat arms, sea trades, aircrew) proficiencies, an understanding and development of the **Military and Organizational** environments, and the practice and eventual stewardship of the profession of arms, with the capacities to represent and transform the system through applications at the **Strategic and Institutional** levels.
COGNITIVE CAPACITIES	Cognitive Capacities consist of: a problem-solving, critical, **Analytic**, "left-brain" competence to think and rationalize with mental discipline in order to draw strong conclusions and make good decisions; plus an innovative, strategic, conceptually **Creative**, "right brain" capacity to find novel means, "outside the box" ends, and previously undiscovered solutions to issues and problems.
SOCIAL CAPACITIES	Social Capacities consist of a sincere and meaningful behavioural **Flexibility** to be all things to all people, combined with **Communications** skills that clarify understanding, resolve conflicts and bridge differences. These capacities are blended with **Interpersonal** proficiency of clarity and persuasiveness, **Team** relationships that create coordination, cohesion, trust and commitment, and **Partnering** capabilities for strategic relations building.

TABLE 2:   THE LEADER FRAMEWORK – FIVE ELEMENTS, SIXTEEN ATTRIBUTES

CHANGE CAPACITIES	Change Capacities involve **Self**-development, with risk and achievement, to ensure self-efficacy, **Group**-directed capacities to ensure unit improvement and group transformation, all with an understanding of the qualities of a CF-wide **Learning Organization**, applications of a learning organization philosophy, and the capacity of strategic knowledge management.
PROFESSIONAL IDEOLOGY	Professional Ideology consists of an acute awareness of the unique, theory-based, discretionary body of knowledge at the core of the profession with an **Internalized Ethos** whose values and beliefs guide the application of that knowledge. The discretionary nature of military knowledge requires keen judgement in its use and involves **Moral Reasoning** in thinking and acting, shaped by the military ethos. Professional Ideology underpins a leader exemplar with **Credibility/Impact** who displays character, openness, assertiveness and extroversion that ensures the necessary effect by and from the leader.

Important to this leader framework development were some practicalities – for the framework of leader elements and attributes to be sufficiently extensive as to be thorough and useful, but not to be so complex as to be incomprehensible and useless in its application. The 16 leader attributes within the taxonomy of 5 leader elements have been constructed accordingly, so as to constitute the *minimum, finite but sufficient* number of such leader components for all military members engaged as leaders, regardless of level, rank, role, goals or responsibilities. The framework design is based on the understanding that the 5 elements and 16 leader attributes will support competency profiling for the primary leader roles and all other leader roles subsequently determined.

The 16 attributes represent the *fundamentally necessary, but not necessarily sufficiently specific* detail for all leadership. These attributes also reflect the "chronology" of some of the elements. For example, Expertise evolves through a career from technical/specialty finesses to a comprehension of military/

organizational wherewithal, and on to a sophistication with experience and seniority of strategic and institutional leader roles and responsibilities. In contrast, Professional Ideology needs to be "front-end loaded" as new CF members are introduced abruptly to military norms and expectations of behaviour, values, respect and commitment, integrated with technical skills training, all as a foundation for worth and professionalism.

The inter-relationship of the five leader elements are best depicted as an assembly of joined puzzle pieces in a schematic that visually represents the interconnectedness and interdependency of the leader elements. Only collectively would the elements make effective leadership possible. Figure 4 reflects that inter-relationship.

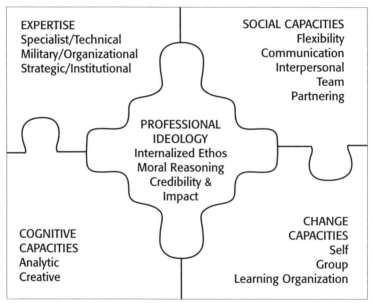

FIGURE 4.   A LEADER FRAMEWORK: 5 LEADER ELEMENTS – 16 LEADER ATTRIBUTES

Readers familiar with leader element taxonomies will recognize the motivational, concise, three-element framework used by the American military, "Be, Know, Do". This "motto" reflects the crucial components of dedicated leadership at all levels for the US forces. As one template for comparison, it dovetails appropriately with the CF leader elements. Figure 5 represents that comparison.

USA	CANADA
BE	To <u>be</u> and to function as professionals through PROFESSIONAL IDEOLOGY
KNOW	To <u>know</u> how to analyze and to create through COGNITIVE CAPACITIES.
	To <u>know</u> how to relate and to explain through SOCIAL CAPACITIES.
	To <u>know</u> how to evolve and to shape change through CHANGE CAPACITIES.
DO	To <u>do</u> specialist, technical, military, organizational, strategic and institutional EXPERTISE.

FIGURE 5.   AMERICAN AND CANADIAN MILITARY TERMINOLOGY: LEADERSHIP

Section 6: The Professional Development Framework

The Professional Development Framework (Figure 6), with a "quartering" of the continuum of leader levels – junior, intermediate, advanced and senior levels – undertaken for explanatory purposes, represents the full template for identifying, defining, and professionally enhancing the leader elements. Figure 6, however, even with a hypothetical progressive professional/leader development process stretched across its frame, is but a skeletal schematic of the leader elements and leader levels of the Professional Development Framework. Table 3 provides substantially more information.

Table 3 reflects that development at the more expansive leader levels – advanced and senior – is founded on development at the less expansive leader levels – junior and intermediate. Additionally, the foci reflect the transition in leadership from a predominantly leading-the-people emphasis at junior and intermediate levels, to a predominantly leading-the-institution commitment at advanced and senior levels.

The content of Table 3 is even more readily comprehended when supplemented by additional descriptive material in this chapter. This text contains several examples and related information relevant to leadership that were extracted from the reports and initiatives of other nations' militaries, and that are crucial as components for a CF Professional Development Framework.

	Expertise	Cognitive Capacities	Social Capacities	Change Capacities	Professional Ideology
Senior	Strategic	Creative Abstract	Inter-Institutional	Paradigm Shifting	Stewardship
Advanced	↑	↑	↑	↑	↑
Intermediate					
Junior	Tactical	Analytical	Inter-Personal	Open	Internalize

FIGURE 6.   THE PROFESSIONAL DEVELOPMENT FRAMEWORK

Expertise has a natural chronology. Early careers are spent with a training focus on military occupational specialties of technical knowledge and expertise. Such specialities are clustered into navy, army and airforce groups such as combat arms, sea trades, or aircrew. With increased leader responsibilities, the relevant expertise must expand into strong military and organizational knowledge, education and information. At advanced and senior leader levels, the expertise is all about strategic wherewithal and institutional wisdom necessary for functioning in a global, multinational security environment while concurrently understanding the machinations of government, political parties, other government departments, as well as the differences between the Department of National Defence and the Canadian Forces.

At these top leader levels, for example, Expertise predominantly consists of the capacities to transform the system through institutional and strategic activities. Knowledge is continually acquired through advanced level courses at national and international institutions, complex self-development, and slow-growth but crucial career experiences. Senior leader expertise would generate consequences such as the necessary operational capacity being met through resource allocation or force structuring, mastery of civil-military relations, and CF-wide transformation oversight. Such Expertise, being knowledge-based, needs to be integrated with cognitive, social and change capacities, and a professional ideology, in order to ensure its effective utilization.

Cognitive Capacities, consisting predominantly of analytical and creative attributes, would require exceptional abilities to analyze, create, diagnose and envision, especially at the most senior leader level. In one relevant study, Australian Eric Stevenson, while examining conceptual complexity capacities across leader levels, researched the differences in mental models, sometimes called cognitive maps, frameworks or mental constructs, between transformational and transactional leaders across the Australian Defence Force (ADF) "trainee, middle and senior" officer levels.[17]

Stevenson proposed that mental models were constructed differently, in terms of structure and sophistication of ideas, between effective and less effective leaders. His study established a significant and positive correlation between effective military officers and well-structured mental models. The content of the mental models differed between transformational and transactional leaders.

Social Capacities for effective leaders include behavioural flexibility and strong communication skills needed at inter-personal, team, and organizational/institutional levels, levels which in themselves represent a continuum of increasing complexity. Factors that contribute even more to this increasing complexity are CF engagements in volatile national and international arenas, with multicultural participants, non-military partners, CF members with well-being

EXPERTISE	
TACTICAL TO STRATEGIC	

LEADER LEVEL	SENIOR	**Security Expertise** • Scope and content moves from knowledge to expertise with accompanying expansion to a strategic understanding of the domain of security. • Shift from knowledge to expertise requires ability to apply the philosophy and principles that govern the generation and employment of military capacities (knowledge + philosophy = expertise) and strategic, institutional co-existence among peer ministries, foreign defence agencies. • Expertise at this stage clearly is dependent upon the complementary development in Professional Ideology, a full understanding of the Profession of Arms.
	ADVANCED	**Defence Knowledge** • From information to knowledge, incorporating a broad understanding of CF and defence as a key component of security and government functions. • Shift from information to knowledge requires additional perspective of understanding the rationale and purpose of intended actions; the generalized outcomes, which are to be achieved (information + purpose = knowledge).
	INTERMEDIATE	**Military Information** • How MOC contributes to larger formation capabilities. • Understanding not only what to do but the context in which this occurs (data + context = information) • Examples: Effects-Based Operations, context of incremental information on democratic systems, international law, civil control of military.
	JUNIOR	**Technical & Tactical Procedures** • Learning standard Military Occupation Classification (MOC) and sea/land/air procedures. • For initial leader roles, acquiring an overview of such standards and procedures, small group tactics.

TABLE 3.   THE PROFESSIONAL DEVELOPMENT FRAMEWORK

		COGNITIVE CAPACITIES ANALYTIC TO CREATIVE/ABSTRACT
LEADER LEVEL	**SENIOR**	**Knowledge Creation** • Able to generate, organize and manage the theory-based body of knowledge applied across the profession. • This goes beyond the analytic, creative and judgement capacities needed to adapt the profession to the external environment, and expands to include the obligation to update and extend the profession's unique body of knowledge to ensure that the profession is discharging all of its responsiblities to society in the most effective manner. • Strong parallel to cognitive capacities at advanced academic post-graduate levels – masters the particular academic discipline but also generated new knowledge.
	ADVANCED	**Mental Models** • Inductive and deductive reasoning skills to create, adapt and generalize knowledge both from one's own previous learning & experiences as well as other domains such as professional literatures. • Conducts abstract reasoning and draws on appropriate professional orientation to be able to understand desired outcomes. • Aware of assumptions embedded in the 'military' way of framing issues, testing working hypotheses, operating within the academic discipline of 'military thinking'.
	INTERMEDIATE	**Theories & Concepts** • Able to reason, moving from the concrete to the abstract, from procedures and rules to principles.
	JUNIOR	**Theorems, Practical Rules** • Reasoning at this level is intended to identify the appropriate task procedures using simple theorems, practical rules or established scientific principles/laws. • Interacting, interconnected with Expertise, the two elements represent a 'cookbook' approach to problem solving and task accomplishment with limited capacity for innovation.

147

| | SOCIAL CAPACITIES |
| | INTERPERSONAL TO INTER-INSTITUTIONAL |

SENIOR

Stratigic-Relations Building

- Relations to the concept of Leading the Institution, relies on secondary and tertiary influence processes for the senior leader to communicate institutional priorities and strategic intent across organizational systems.
- Builds open teams such that immediate subordinates can contribute novel ideas and can critique taken-for-granted assumptions.
- Externally focused capacities pertain to building and maintaining strategic relations with others engaged in the broad security arena and related national/governmental initiatives.

ADVANCED

Group Cohesiveness

- At this level of larger or multiple unite/team/groups, is involved in aspects of Leading the Institution, applies broad influence processes to ensure internal cohesion, fostering commitment and supporting subordinate leaders while also engaging in effective boundary spanning activities especially in joint or multi-national operations.

INTERMEDIATE

Individual Persuasion

- Social skills for Leading People, particularly the abilities to effectively influence others 'one-to-one' or small-group, using some range of influence behaviours appropriate to the characteristics of the situation, the followers and the individual leader.

JUNIOR

Team-Oriented Followship

- Aware of group norms, minimum leader style flexibility.
- Moderate communication· capabilities applied through baseline interpersonal skills reflecting an awareness of basic influence factors, group diversity issues and non-prejudicial self-behaviour.

LEADER LEVEL

		CHANGE CAPACITIES
		OPENNESS TO PARADIGM SHIFTING

Multi-Institutional Partnering

- Focus is external, on changing others' understanding of the military as a strategic political capacity, and internally on implementing internal change initiatives.
- In this latter regard, there is an emphasis on the initial stages of anticipating change, effectively contributing to the change, and monitoring and adjusting initiatives over the change period.
- Senior leader initiatives exist to transform and improve a team or multiple units, or to attempt learning-organization applications at organizational and institutional levels.

Group Transformation

- Able to adapt and align groups or sub-systems to the broadest requirements of the institution while ensuring the tactical proficiency and effective integration of individuals and small teams/sections within the larger formation.

Self-Efficacy

- Capacities at this stage are focused on the individual's abilities to monitor self-efficacy, engage in self-reflection, make early commitments to self-development, and adapt one's behaviours to the social environment/context in which one is functioning.

External Awareness

- Minimal expectation in change capacities would be a generalized orientation and awareness of changes occurring enternal to the CF, and the CF transformational efforts, as means of signalling the importance of practicing openness to externally-driven change.

LEADER LEVEL — SENIOR / ADVANCED / INTERMEDIATE / JUNIOR

		PROFESSIONAL IDEOLOGY INTERNALIZING TO STEWARDSHIP
LEADER LEVEL	**SENIOR**	**Stewardship of the Profession** • Core capacities are related to managing collective professional identity – the key issue of articulating what the profession is, what it stands for and what it believes in. • Able to engage in very abstract reasoning, exemplifies at the highest stages of moral/identity development, in particular, the capacity for independent judgement of the profession's core philosophy, ideology and principles. • This capacity is integrated with acquisition of related capabilities in Cognitive and Change Capacities.
	ADVANCED	**Cultural Alignment** • Guides framing of problems, interactions with others, to apply leader influence to shape or align the extant culture to be consistent with the ethos. • Contains some of the most complex challenges in achieving competing Institutional Effectiveness objectives – mission success versus member well-being; internal synchrony and stability versus external adaptability and experimentation.
	INTERMEDIATE	**Self-Regulation** • Conducts basic self-regulation, avoiding obvious ethical violations and not displaying behaviours which erode the reputation, image or credibility of the profession; essentially a journeyman stage of prefessionalization. • Abides by the principles of the Defence Ethics Program. • Capable of serving as an example.
	JUNIOR	**Normative Compliance** • Understands the concepts and practices of the profession of arms at an introductory level. At a minimum practices military group norms, adheres to discipline demands. • As an *ab initio* professional (apprentice), looks externally (to supervisors or codes of conduct) for guidance as to the appropriate behaviours in specific circumstances. Internalizes values minimally.

concerns versus unlimited-liability responsibilities, and culturally diverse civilian partners as well as CF recruits. Leaders need the social capacities to be flexible in their leader roles, always with authenticity and sincerity. That flexibility in roles would allow differentiation needed to work with different groups, cultures, nationalities, but that flexibility also must be sufficiently consistent so that a syndrome of imposture or deception is not perceived in error.

An example of current research on social capacities was done by American researchers Michael Mumford and colleagues.[18] They studied social skills and cognitive skills over six grade levels of US military officers in order to create an organization-based model of skill development. They established that it was insufficient for leaders to just solve ill-defined and complex organizational problems. Leaders required as well, the social capacities to formulate solutions in complex organizational environments that were workable in accordance with the multiple constitutencies represented by diverse people. They coined the term "complex organizational wisdom" for the social capacities that could be developed through mentoring by senior leaders, novel assignments, solving problems requiring the respondent's autonomy, risk-taking, sequential and updated environmental assessments, and long-term solutions for the multiple subsystems.

Change Capacities for leaders include the first step of self-development to ensure self-efficacy, non-risk-aversion and experimentation, even before any leader takes initiatives to transform and improve a team or unit, or to attempt learning-organization applications at organizational and institutional levels. A cluster of West Point-affiliated leadership experts, George Forsythe, Paul Bartone and others[19] utilized Robert Kegan's[20] theory of identity development to study how much officers understood who they were as military professionals. They explored the way that officers think across junior to senior levels, how they "make meaning", particularly with respect to the American "Be, Know, Do" framework for leader development, and how they evolve from single perspectives at young ages, to multiple perspectives with maturity, on to simultaneous multiple perspectives and, at the fourth Kegan stage, to have constructed a personal perspective on relationships and societal ideals. They observed that this fourth stage of Kegan's Identity Development scale (a self-authored system of values; personal perspective on relationships and societal ideals; independence from the existing institution) may be required to truly lead a profession, as opposed to being just a member imbedded within it.

Professional Ideology occupies a privileged position in the Professional Development Framework. The other four elements of the Framework – Expertise, Cognitive Capacities, Social Capacities, Change Capacities - are present in most effective organizations. Only when these elements are shaped by a Professional Ideology (depicted in Figure 6 as concentric rings, like an old-fashioned sonar burst) do all five elements coalesce into a collective, interdependent, "Rubik's Cube" of effective leader elements needed for achieving complete institutional effectiveness.

Significantly, Professional Ideology claims a unique, discretionary, theory-based body of military knowledge authoritative in a functional and cognitive sense, along with a military ethos that guides and adjudicates how that knowledge is used. The theory-based knowledge consists of the General System of War and Conflict comprising policy, strategy, operational art and tactics. The military ethos consists of three components: Beliefs and Expectations about Military Service; Fundamental Canadian Values; and the Core Military Values, as articulated in *Duty with Honour*. Professional Ideology demands doing good work over self-interest, and effectiveness over efficiency. A professional ideology stands in contrast to a bureaucratic ideology with its "ethos" of managerialism and a market ideology with its "ethos" of entrepreneurialism.

THE OUTCOMES – THE SUCCESSES

Section 7: Applications and Feedback

Referring once more to Figure 1, the confluence within the flowchart of the institution, as depicted by the CF Effectiveness model, and the CF leadership as depicted by the Professional Development Framework, has generated the institution-leadership congruence required and pursued for successful CF Applications. With leadership becoming increasingly complex as the 21st century progresses, effective CF leadership requires strong and diverse capacities and attributes. The relevance of the Professional Development Framework to generate these capacities and, therefore, to ensure the institutional effectiveness of the CF, is best exemplified through real-time and current applications.

To demonstrate that the Professional Development Framework is relevant and applicable at all levels of the institution and the leadership, six current CF Applications, consisting of micro through macro examples, are described in detail, below:

- The applicability of 360° assessment feedback to individual leader development;

- The senior CF leaders contingent's professional development needs and challenges;

- Effective professional development methodologies and learning strategies;

- Review and reform in the CF's current human resources/personnel systems;

- Evolving operational leader challenges in warfighting, while nation building;

- CF Transformation, six CDS Principles, and the Professional Development Framework.

360° Assessment Feedback. The argument is that institutional effectiveness for an organization can be attained if the requisite leader capacities necessary for institutional effectiveness are present and applied. Leader capacities do benefit from professional development, of which one methodology is self-development. (Self-development is a foundational attribute of the Change Capacities element of the Professional Development Framework.) One outcome of self-development is self-awareness, and one means for acquiring self-awareness is valid feedback from a variety of "stakeholders", of professional colleagues, which in the CF would be superiors, peers, subordinates and other working colleagues inside and outside the CF. One effective means for acquiring valid feedback on leader behaviours, strengths and shortcomings, is a well-designed and well-conducted multi-rater 360° feedback process with professional debriefs and appropriate follow-up, support, and guidelines for personal/professional development.

As an example, the Canadian Forces College (CFC) has utilized self-report assessment processes with senior officers to enhance their self-awareness and focus on personal development. In 2003, CFC expanded student assessment processes to include completion of 360° assessment feedback inventories and provision of developmental feedback. The procedures became a course requirement for officers attending the annual Command and Staff Course (CSC).[21] A context-specific 360° feedback instrument, adequately encapsulating the Professional Development Framework's five leader elements, was specifically designed for the CSC mid-level leaders.

Senior Leader Professional Development. The professional development needs of senior leaders were identified through a substantial research effort, including a thorough analysis of the suite of 2020 CF documents, other military sources, and the generic leadership literature. Recent interviews by CFLI with senior officers and NCOs underscored the need for ongoing development,[22] but also revealed unique challenges for senior leader professional development.[23] Contrasted with valid and well-founded needs articulated by senior military members for increased breadth, depth and time for senior leader development was the absence of availability and time among these same senior leaders. Any learning initiative, therefore, needed to be convenient and succinct, with no time wasted and limited time "lost" at the office. Solutions would exist only through selection of the most beneficial subject matter and the most appropriate learning strategies.

Not surprisingly, the areas for professional development for senior officers identified by CF senior officers fit appropriately into the Professional Development Framework. As examples, for advanced and senior leaders focusing on institutional leadership, increased emphasis on adult-learning strategies would be most appropriate to develop top-level leader elements in the Professional Development Framework. Examples are professional Expertise related to institutional and strategic capabilities (e.g., understanding and influencing "how Ottawa works"), Cognitive Capacities (e.g., complex organizational wisdom, innovative thinking), Social Capacities (e.g., leader flexibility, effective communication when partnering with international organizations), Change Capacities (e.g., learning-organization information-sharing applicable to simultaneous warfighting and nation building), and Professional Ideology (e.g., proactively, beyond osmosis, becoming exemplars, custodians, stewards of the profession, using moral/ethical reasoning, balancing autonomous thinking with conformity to team norms and membership, etc.). Subject matter that would pull together these learning foci could include: Stewarding the Profession, "Understanding Ottawa" and "Working the Town", Visioning, Leading & Implementing Change, Being a Strategic Leader, Personalities in Cabinet, Integrating the Major Internal Systems, Advancing Member Well-Being & Commitment, or Creating the Effective Institutional Leader.

With extensive senior service and significant experience also comes the need for professional development to establish a deeper, inculcated and complex Professional Ideology. This Professional Ideology, having been important from the outset of a military career, needs to be expanded and continued throughout that military career in line with the increasingly more senior responsibility for institutional and strategic roles.

<u>Professional Development Strategies for Leader Capacities</u>. Until recent years, through the industrial era and until the end of the Cold War, leadership research and leadership development had focused almost exclusively on generally circumscribed and static leader-situation-follower scenarios. The pedagogical approach – teacher-centred information dissemination - for the professional development of these leadership circumstances reflected this restrictive focus.

With a more complex world has come a more complex perspective, one with great expectations for senior leaders to manage and shape perpetual change in a professional manner. The need is for dynamic solutions through leading that change, leading the institution, and influencing the external environment. As Figure 3, above, indicated, the transition from the industrial to the information eras has included a worksite transformation from a work orientation to a worker/leader orientation, this being one major cause behind that expectation for dynamic solutions. These are the circumstances of the new information era, for which expanded and effective CF leader development strategies and methodologies are crucial.

Capt(N) Jennifer Bennett, author of this book's Chapter 8, provides a substantial and thorough discourse on the current and urgent need for improved learning strategies and methods that would support the acquisition by CF leaders of superior leader capacities. With leadership described as a taxonomy of clusters of interconnected requisite capacities, the enhancement of leadership as an institutional requirement is best addressed through a variety of leader development methodologies. As per chapter 8, proven "best practices" for learning systems are needed now.

<u>CF Human Resources Systems Reform</u>. The importance of reform of CF HR systems was addressed extensively in Chapter 7, "Ensuring Effective Succession of Institutional Leaders", of *Leadership in the Canadian Forces: Leading the Institution*. The subject will be reviewed briefly here in relationship to the relevant application of the Professional Development Framework.

Senior leaders are policy overseers, strategic decision-makers and executive communicators, utilizing their sophisticated awareness of human capacities and human resources (HR) systems to ensure that these systems are current and effective. Examples of such systems are the recruiting/selection system, performance appraisal and promotion, HR management and career management, and succession planning.[24] The Professional Development Framework, as the instrument for categorizing the requisite human/leader capacities, can act as a conceptual foundation for reviewing and restructuring current HR policies, programs and procedures, hence the Framework is important to leaders of the institution. Applying this framework of capacities to the different HR programs and procedures would improve them and increase their relevance.[25] Some of the broader HR policy implications can be:

- Recruiting and Selection. The existing CF entry-level recruiting and selection model is based primarily on identifying those most likely to complete initial technical training, using previous academic performance and general learning ability, as well as previous "reliability" behaviours to screen out those unlikely to adapt successfully to military training and lifestyles. The Professional Development Framework supports a more comprehensive model for recruiting and selection through incorporating, and assessing, moral reasoning, identity development, balancing autonomous thinking with conformity, and assessing the propensity to inculcate a professional ideology.

- Performance Appraisal & Promotion. Performance appraisal, when used for promotion decisions, is simply another selection process applied to the eligible internal population of contenders. The Professional Development Framework provides a broader conceptual basis to identify significant and meaningful discontinuities in capacities from one rank to the next or one leader level to the next.

- Career Management. The Professional Development Framework is applicable in circumstances demanding significantly different leader attributes and capacities, such as circumstances with competing institutional outcomes, e.g., mission success versus member well-being, and internal organizational stability versus shaping change to ensure external adaptability. Career management systems would need senior members and administrators capable of identifying and discriminating among the crucial qualities and capacities of senior leaders. (As stated elsewhere, think cool Colin Powell versus Stormin' Norman Schwartzkopf, Gulf War I, 1990s! Think, too, of the dynamics of leadership, had these two individuals had, instead, the responsibilities of each other's positions!)

- Succession Planning. An integrated "leading the institution" philosophy is mandatory in the effective coordination of any organization's succession planning requirements. Only with complete development of upcoming successors in the leader domains identified in the Professional Development Framework can an HR succession planning system work. That system must ensure that the very best institutional leaders will inherit the responsibilities to effectively transform the CF and lead it further into the 21st century.

Effective leadership, as captured in the Professional Development Framework, is possible through the presence of current, interconnected, requisite expertise and capacities. The leader's professional ideology, being far more than a sense of right-mindedness and a list of positive attributes, will pervade all of this leader expertise and the cognitive, social and change capacities. Ensuring that the right members in the right positions at the right levels with the right responsibilities is achievable and implementable through modernized and flexible HR processes that incorporate the Professional Development Framework.

Operational Leader Challenges While Nation Building. As stated above in Section 4, Canadian Forces Leader Issues, current CF member deployments in Afghanistan reflect the most recent and tragic complexities in leadership challenges. CFLI's Director, Colonel Bernd Horn,[26] through research in Afghanistan, identified unique tactical, operational and strategic leadership challenges evolving from the singular characteristics of leading soldiers in an Afghan version of the "three block war" - warfighting, conflict resolution, and nation building through humanitarian endeavours. Horn described:

- tactical level leadership as requiring a mix of the maintaining of a fighting spirit and a sustained morale, facing the realities of fleeting and deadly attacks unable to be proactively anticipated, sustaining a healthy outlook among soldiers toward the general population while difficulty exists to breach the cultural barriers, and overseeing action-oriented tactical leadership while also continually improving upon working relationships with the host nation's forces and citizens;

- at the operational level of leadership, the challenge begins with generating a comprehensive understanding by all members of the nature of fourth generation warfare (which Horn defines as a nonlinear, asymmetric approach to war in which agility, decentralization and initiative are instrumental to success) and, specifically, the nature of the insurgency that grips Afghanistan, complicated by the reality that the resolution of political and economic issues being far more critical to success than purely military action; and

- the achievement of strategic goals only through the vehicle of an effective campaign plan that in itself is a difficult balancing act requiring agile thinking, flexible conduct, distributed leadership and decentralized initiatives, and with a culture among military members/followers of similar adaptability, agility of thought, and timely decision-making, all in an ambiguous, complex and lethal environment. Simultaneously, strategic leaders must ensure national support from a Canadian public, maintain a sustained war effort without alienating taxpayers nor losing their support as casualties increase, and adopting the 3D diplomacy-development-defence approach at a national level.

Afghanistan represents the volatile, unpredictable, complex and multi-layered challenges of an ambiguous operational theatre for CF leaders at all levels. These challenges demand truth, duty and valour in its individual leaders leading people, and tenacity, decisiveness and versatility in its leader corps leading the CF institution. These challenges demand highly developed leader capacities as represented in the Professional Development Framework – newfound expertise for a 3D theatre, cognitive capacities that respond to the flexible and immediate demands for decision-making, flexible social capacities to communicate this complexity to the fighting forces and to respond with alacrity to the cultural, political and diplomatic requirements of the job, and a professionalism of character and morality that reflects Canadian and CF values. Once again, this Framework has substantial relevance to institutional effectiveness for the CF, in this case in a foreign operational warfighting arena demanding exceptional tactical, operational and strategic leadership.

CF Transformation, CDS Principles and the Professional Development Framework. The Professional Development Framework was designed for appicability across the micro-to-macro CF circumstances of leadership. At the macro, institution-wide, level, the Framework has substantial applicability for the current CF Transformation (2005 and on)[27] in which the CDS' vision includes changing the way the CF is structured and equipped, and its members trained and educated, in order to execute military missions.

At the heart of this vision is a new focus on Canada as an operational theatre like any other operational theatre, organized and commanded by one joint force commander as opposed to a number of command arrangements existing from previous historical developments. Within this strategic context, the CDS has identified six key principles applicable to the transformation efforts and to guide the success of this mission of transformation.[28] These principles will guide the reshaping and renewal of CF culture and will create a shared ethos fundamental to a CF that is relevant, responsive and effective in an increasingly unstable and complex strategic environment. Not surprisingly, recently created CF professional and leadership doctrine in CF manuals *Duty with Honour* and *Leadership in the Canadian Forces: Conceptual Foundations* fully supports this new agenda. In addition, the Professional Development Framework substantiates a system of professional development to meet the CF professionalism and leadership requirements for this CF transformation to ensure mission success in an ever-changing and deadly battlespace.

The six principles identified by the CDS are:

- Canadian Forces Identity. The first loyalty is to Canada. Service personnel must look beyond their environments and unit affiliations to identify with the CF "holistically" and to serve Canada with commitment.

- Command Centric Imperative. To establish a distinct and unambiguous chain of command that integrates strategic, operational, and tactical decision-making throughout the CF, and clearly separates line and staff functions.

- Authorities, Responsibilities, and Accountabilities. Commanders receive a clear articulation of their assigned authorities, responsibilities, and accountabilities. In turn, they can provide equal clarity in their guidance to subordinate commanders.

- Operational Focus. Operations and operational support has primacy over all other activities within the CF, particularly at the strategic level where departmental, corporate and CF priorities intersect.

- <u>Mission Command.</u> In essence, mission command articulates the dynamic and decentralized execution of CF operations, guided by a clear articulation and understanding of the overriding commander's intent. Permits discretionary powers within the commander's intent at the lowest levels in the battlespace.

- <u>An Integrated Regular, Reserve and Civilian CF.</u> Encourages a more integrated effort where CF structures are closely interconnected and interdependent, to ensure the best utilization of appropriate skills and experiences at every level.

CF leaders can accomplish these ambitious plans for transformation through leadership effectiveness and its development as identified in the Professional Development Framework. The Framework fully supports the transformation principles by substantiating initiatives that include broadly based leader development to address the technical expertise and military developments that require cognitive capacities such as accelerated decision-making, more innovative initiatives, and coordinated but individualistic creativity highly valued across the spectrum of operations. Distributed leadership doctrine and the social capacities of leaders to ensure such leadership will improve the probabilities that every member will accept responsibility for the mission and the effectiveness of the team, the unit, multi-units and, ultimately, the CF. The change capacities in the Professional Development Framework are crucial to timely and effective responses to volatile current battlespaces and to shaping change in order to generate more favourable circumstances in future battle sites and support networks.

<u>Feedback</u>. Section 7, Applications and Feedback, identified six successful outcomes following from the effective congruence of the CF as an institution with its leadership. These applications are successful examples of the model and structure of Institutional/CF Effectiveness on one side of the Congruence equation, and effective leadership represented by the Professional Development Framework on the other side of the Congruence equation (Figure 1). The six

applications ranged from micro-to-macro examples – individual 360° feedback, senior leaders' professional development, learning strategies and methodologies, human resources systems reform, battlespace leader challenges, and CF transformation.

Feedback is crucial to the perpetual improvement of transformations, CF missions, operating systems, unit or team capacities, or individual capabilities. Accordingly, the schematic described at Figure 1 includes feedback loops that follow from the Applications and influence the other components of the flow chart. The CF will be in a state of perpetual flux, regardless of current or future transformation initiatives, due to its need for survival through its external adaptability, its successive fine-tuning and internal integration of its components, its investment in its members' well-being and commmitment, and its life-or-death investment in the success of its missions.

SUMMARY

Effectiveness for any institutional has the potential to be achieved if certain specifics are addressed. The roles and responsibilities of the leaders of an institution need to be articulated. The leader capacities necessary to achieve those roles and responsibilities need to be identified. For the CF as an institution, those capacities have been integrated into a construct of leader elements and leader attributes. Further, these leader capacities have been stretched over a continuum of leader levels, from junior to senior, to reflect the evolution of such capacities with evolving responsibilities.

The Professional Development Framework consists of a table of 5x4 cells representing the five leader elements over four leader levels. When, in addition, the most effective learning strategies for these elements and levels are integrated and utilized, the Framework becomes a comprehensive model for expanding the depth and breadth of leadership, professionalism and leader development. The Professional Development Framework supports a shift from a pedagogical sufficiency ("pass") model of development to a mastery ("excel") model of performance, human resourcing, professionalism and leadership. This shift supports the identification of the professionally developed military leaders with the highest potential, rather than simply those military members fundamentally suited for their next appointments.

The overriding and continuous theme for the CF is *Transformation*. This transformation needs to be, must be, accomplished by a focus on its people – members in the CF professionally enhanced in their leader capacities sufficiently to master all of the challenges of the 21st century.

The Professional Development Framework is a crucial linchpin for this overall effort.[29]

SELECT BIBLIOGRAPHY

Horn, B. (ed.) *Contemporary Issues in Officership: A Canadian Perspective.* Toronto: Canadian Institute of Strategic Studies, 2000.

Horn, B. & Harris, S. J (eds.) *Generalship and the Art of the Admiral: Perspectives on Canadian Senior Military Leadership.* St. Catharines: Vanwell Publishing Limited, 2001.

Hughes, R. L. & Beatty, K. C. *Becoming a Strategic Leader.* San Francisco, CA: Jossey-Bass and Centre for Creative Leadership, 2005.

Shambach, S. (ed.) *Strategic Leadership. Primer* Carlisle Barracks, Pennsylvania: Department of Command, Leadership and Management, US Army War College, 2004 at www.carlisle.army/mil/dclm/.

Ulmer, W. F. Jr., "Military Leadership into the 21st Century: Another "Bridge Too Far"?" *Parameters*, Spring 1998, 4-25. Carlisle Barracks, Pennsylvania: US Army War College, 1998.

Wong, L., Gerras, S., Kidd, W., Pricone, R., Swengros, R. *Strategic Leadership Competencies.* Carlisle Barracks, Pennsylvania: Strategic Studies Institute, US Army War College, 2003 at www.carlisle.army/mil/ssi/pubs/.

Walker, R. W., *The Professional Development Framework: Generating Effectiveness in Canadian Forces Leaders*, CFLI Technical Report 2006-01. Kingston, ON: Canadian Forces Leadership Institute, 2006 at www.cda-acd.forces.gc.ca/cfli.

Wenek, K. W. J., "Defining Leadership". Unpublished Paper. Kingston, ON: Canadian Forces Leadership Institute, 2003 at www.cda-acd.forces.gc.ca/cfli/research papers.

Wenek, K. W. J., "Defining Effective Leadership in the Canadian Forces", Unpublished Paper. Kingston, ON: Canadian Forces Leadership Institute, 2003 at www.cda-acd.forces.gc.ca/cfli/research papers.

Yukl, G. "Leadership Competencies Required for the New Army and Approaches for Developing Them," in James Hunt, George Dodge, & Leonard Wong (eds.), *Out-of-the-Box Leadership: Transforming the Twenty-First Century Army and Other Top-Performing Organizations*. Stamford, CT: JAI Press, 1999.

Zaccaro, S. *The Nature of Executive Leadership: A Conceptual and Empirical Analysis of Success*. Washington, DC: American Psychological Association, 2001.

ENDNOTES

1   Karol W. J. Wenek, "Institutional Challenge and Change in the 21st Century: The Road Ahead for Canadian Forces Leadership", Presentation at Armed Forces and Society (IUS) Conference, Kingston, Canada, October 2002; "Looking Back: Canadian Forces Leadership Problems and Challenges", Unpublished Paper (Kingston, ON: CF Leadership Institute, 2002); "Looking Ahead: Contexts of Canadian Forces Leadership Today and Tomorrow", Unpublished Paper (Kingston, ON: CF Leadership Institute, 2002); "Defining Leadership", Unpublished Paper (Kingston, ON: CF Leadership Institute, 2003); and "Defining Effective Leadership in the Canadian Forces", Unpublished Paper (Kingston, ON: CF Leadership Institute, 2003), unpublished papers at www.cda-acd.forces.gc.ca/cfli/research papers.

2   Scot Robertson and Michael Hennessy, "The Canadian Forces of Tomorrow: Maintaining Strategic Effectiveness and Relevance in the 21st Century," *Canadian Military Journal*, Volume 4, Number 1,

Spring, 2003, 54-56; *Future Force: Concepts for Future Army Capabilities* (Kingston, ON: Canadian Forces Directorate of Land Strategic Concepts, 2003).

3   Canada. *Leadership in the Canadian Forces: Conceptual Foundations* (Kingston, ON: Canadian Forces Leadership Institute, 2005). Table 4-1, Functional Responsibilities of CF Leaders, pages 48-49, at www.cda-acd.forces.gc.ca/cfli.

4   T. Owen Jacobs and Elliot Jaques, "Military Executive Leadership," in K. Clark & M. Clark, *Measures of Leadership* (Greensboro, N.C., Center for Creative Leadership, 1990).

5   Robert E. Quinn, *Beyond Rational Management: Mastering the Paradoxes and Competing Demands of High Performance* (San Francisco: Jossey-Bass, 1988); and Kim Cameron and Robert E. Quinn, *Diagnosing & Changing Organizational Culture* (New York: Addison Wesley, 1999). *Leadership in the Canadian Forces: Conceptual Foundations*, Chapter 2, Annex A (see Figure 2A-1) explains Quinn's Framework and how a CF-context institutional effectiveness model was created as an organizationally specific adaptation of the generic model.

6   Summarized in B. J. Hodge and W. P. Anthony, *Organisational Theory: A Strategic Approach*, 4th ed. (Boston: Allyn & Bacon, 1991).

7   Robert E. Quinn, *Beyond Rational Management*, 31.

8   Bernd Horn, "'Outside the Wire' – Some CF Leadership Challenges in Afghanistan", *Canadian Military Journal*, Volume 7, Number 3, Fall 2006.

9   Shaun Newsome, Arla L. Day, and Victor M. Catano, "Leader Assessment, Evaluation and Development", CFLI Contract Research Report #CR01-0094. (Kingston, ON: Canadian Forces Leadership Institute, 2002).

10   Wenek, "Defining Effective Leadership", 39.

11   Stephen Zaccaro, *The Nature of Executive Leadership: A Conceptual and Empirical Analysis of Success* (Washington, DC: American Psychological Association, 2001).

12   Wenek, "Defining Effective Leadership", 31.

13   Sources for Table 1: Public Service executive competencies, (Canada's Public Service Commission, 1999); Gary Yukl, "Leadership Competencies Required for the New Army and Approaches for Developing Them," in James Hunt, George Dodge, & Leonard Wong, eds., *Out-of-the-Box Leadership: Transforming the Twenty-First Century Army and Other Top-Performing Organizations* (Stamford, CT: JAI Press, 1999); Gardner's leader attributes, in J. H. Boyett & J. T. Boyett, *The Guru Guide: The Best Ideas of the Top Management Thinkers* (New York:

John Wiley & Sons, 1990); *Tett's Leadership Competencies* referenced in "Leader Assessment, Evaluation and Development" by Shaun Newsome, Arla L. Day, and Victor M. Catano, CFLI Contract Research Report #CR01-0094 (Kingston, ON: Canadian Forces Leadership Institute, 2002); Lyle M. Spencer & Signe M. Spencer, *Competence at Work: Models for Superior Performance* (New York: John Wiley & Sons, 1993).

14   Alan Okros, Karol W. J. Wenek, and Robert W. Walker, "A Rational Model of Leader Development", Presentation at the Annual Conference of the Canadian Psychological Association, Hamilton, ON, June 2003.

15   Karol W. J. Wenek, personal communication, 12 September 2003.

16   Karol W. J. Wenek, Unpublished draft material for *Leadership in the Canadian Forces: Conceptual Foundations*, April 2004.

17   Eric Stevenson, "Command Presence: Australian Military Officers' Mental Model of Effective Leaders" (School of Economics and Management, University College, Australian Defence Force Academy). Unpublished Paper. Undated.

18   Michael D. Mumford, Michelle A. Marks, Mary Shane Connelly, Stephen J. Zaccaro, and Roni Reiter-Palmon. "Development of Leadership Skills – Experience and Timing". *Leadership Quarterly*, 11(1), 2000, 87-114.

19   George B. Forsythe, Scott Snook, Philip Lewis, and Paul T. Bartone, "Making Sense of Officership: Developing a Professional Identity for 21st Century Army Officers". In Lloyd J. Mathews, ed., Don M. Snider & Gayle L. Watkins, project directors, *The Future of the Army Profession*. (Boston: McGraw-Hill, 2002).

20   Robert Kegan, *The Evolving Self: Problem and Process in Human Development* (Cambridge: Harvard University Press, 1982).

21   Robert W. Walker and Marjory Kerr, "Leadership, Professional Development and Self-Awareness, A 360° Feedback Project". Paper presented at the Annual Conference of the Canadian Psychological Association, St. John's, Newfoundland and Labrador, June 2004.

22   Robert W. Walker, "The Canadian Forces Leader Framework: Senior Leader Attributes and the Requisite Professional Development to Enhance Them". Paper presented at the Annual Conference of the Canadian Psychological Association, Montreal, Quebec, June 2005.

23   Robert W. Walker, L. William Bentley, and Bernd Horn, "Senior Leaders Project – Professional Development" (Kingston, ON: Canadian Forces Leadership Institute, 2005), Discussion Paper at www.cda-acd.forces.gc.ca/cfli.

24   Canada. *Leadership in the Canadian Forces: Leading the Institution* (Kingston, ON: Canadian Forces Leadership Institute, 2006). Section 3, Building Institutional Leadership, Chapter 7, Ensuring Effective Succession of Institutional Leadership.

25   Alan Okros, "Applying the CFLI Leader Framework" (Kingston, ON: Royal Military College, Department of Military Psychology and Leadership, 2004). Unpublished Paper. Dr. Okros' ideas are paraphrased here with his permission.

26   Horn, "'Outside the Wire'".

27   Robert S. Edwards, L. William Bentley, L. W. and Robert W. Walker, "Professionalism and Leadership: Requisite Proficiencies for CF Transformation," *Canadian Military Journal*, Volume 7, No. 1, Spring 2006, 6-12.

28   CFLI is initiating the production of a book, *Inside CF Transformation 2005-2007*, for publication in 2007. It will be a historical review of the restructuring of the CF. This case study, in addition to providing a general, historical overview of institutional development and change, can serve as an instrument of professional leader development through dynamic learning simulations, future after-action reviews, and "lessons learned" syndicate exercises in the CF. This publication also can serve private industry and government departments as they engage in comparisons of institutions undergoing transformations.

29   This chapter is a partial distillation of the Canadian Forces Leadership Institute's Technical Report 2006-01 authored by Robert W. Walker and titled *The Professional Development Framework: Generating Effectiveness in Canadian Forces Leaders*, (Kingston, ON:). That report can be found at www.cda–acd.forces.gc.ca/cfli.

CHAPTER EIGHT

EFFECTIVE PROFESSIONAL DEVELOPMENT STRATEGIES FOR INSTITUTIONAL LEADERS

Captain(N) Jennifer J. Bennett

In the past, military leaders have relied upon a combination of technical skills, thinking skills and interpersonal skills, the majority of which were acquired through training and experience. While these skills were suitable in the Cold War era, this is no longer the case. In a global environment where change is the only constant, successful organizations need to ensure their leaders are adaptable, innovative and knowledgeable.

The leaders of today's Canadian Forces not only lead the members of the organization but the institution itself. Senior military leaders now need a wider range of competencies and attributes that allow them to effectively achieve mission success, internal integration, external adaptability, and member well-being and commitment in the profession of arms.[1]

The challenges of a new operational and corporate environment have called into question the effectiveness of past professional development practices and programs. Leadership development does not end with graduation from the final formal development period, a senior appointment or promotion. Senior leaders of the CF must continue to learn and to seek professional development opportunities that enhance not only their ability to perform their miltiary duties but to provide more effective leadership to the institution.

This has necessitated the consideration of a wider range of professional development methods to enhance senior leader effectiveness and their ability to make the transition from predominantly leading people, to positions of senior leadership that include leading the institution.

169

Although the CF has developed a comprehensive model of professional development that includes self-development, experience, training and education, efforts have been concentrated on predominantly *pedagogical* (teacher led) methodologies and leadership development up to the executive or senior level. The pedagogical model assigns the teacher full responsibility for making all decisions about what will be learned, how it will be learned, and if it has been learned. This is typical of our current CF training system and many of our courses are designed and delivered based on this model. While this method has advantages for certain subject areas, it is teacher-directed and places the learner in a submissive role following the teacher's instructions and lead.

Until very recently, the pedagogical model has been applied equally to the teaching of children and adults, and in a sense, is a contradiction in terms. The reason is that as adults mature, they become increasingly independent and responsible for their own actions. They are often motivated to learn by a sincere desire to solve immediate problems in their lives and adults have an increasing need to be self-directing. In many ways, the CF pedagogical model of training and professional development does not account for developmental changes in adults, and thus may be cause for tension, resentment, and resistance in individuals within the more regimented training system, particularly more senior and experienced CF members.

A recent research study conducted with senior DND and CF leaders confirmed that a more holistic, *andragogical* (student led) approach that includes effective assessment and feedback tools, mentoring, a CF leader framework, more frequent rotations through headquarters, flexible terms of service and increased early opportunities for varied responsibilities that support leader development across a military career would enhance professional development of senior CF leaders.

In the past, the priorities of the CF training and education system were preparing members for operations and the leadership of people. While there are a wealth of learning opportunities up to the senior leader level, professional development suddenly tapers off just at the time when responsibility and expectations are at their maximum. Learning should be progressive and life-long, not tied to a certain stage, grade, level or developmental period. Professional development should be continuous across a career and go beyond the classroom or school settings associated with formal courses.

Several Canadian Forces strategic documents – *Strategy 2020, Officership 2020, Non-Commissioned Member 2020 (NCM Corps 2020), Military Human Resources Strategy 2020 (HR Strategy 2020)* - supported by past lessons learned and gap analyses have identified the need for a more proactive approach to senior leader development, including a professional development model that introduces the concept of leading the institution earlier; more effective succession planning and career development with personal development plans; utilization of a variety of means of professional development; use of a wider range of performance measurement including 360° evaluations; and earlier introduction of professional ideology.[2]

Research and literature on adult learning and learning styles is consistent and clear in recommending that methods of instructions, professional development and education for adults provide 'active learning' and discovery as opposed to 'passive instruction'. Malcolm Knowles, the first in North America to use the term 'androgogy', offers sound reasons for this approach to adult education when he cites the evidence that those who take initiative in their education and associated activities seem to learn more and learn things better than those who were passive participants in merely receiving information.[3] Knowles observed that as we mature, we strive to take on increasing responsibility for life[4] and the same is true of our professional development. The most relevant to learning organizations such as the CF is the observation that education delivery methods in general continue to evolve to more 'learner centric' approaches including distance learning, e-learning and self-directed learning where the learner must assume not only more responsibility but more initiative for their learning.

The literature and research on adult learning and learning styles is also consistent with the literature on strategic leadership development in suggesting that the most effective methods of professional development are interactive and should focus more on the process and less on the content. Strategies that have proven to be effective with executive leaders include case studies, role-playing, simulations, coaching, syndicate discussions and self-evaluation/reflection.

While CF professional development is currently structured upon more formal learning opportunities (courses, assignments and evaluation processes), these are gradually being augmented and adjusted to acknowledge the many informal learning opportunities that occur naturally in the workplace. These opportunities are extremely useful as they are timely, adaptive, on-site and need-specific. However, because they have not been part of our formal development process, they have not necessarily been considered as professional development *per se*. Introducing a wider range of methodologies of professional development across the CF professional development system will facilitate the creation of a more diverse learning environment that will see professional development that is not only modern, innovative, flexible, timely and, most important, practical, but an integral part of our day-to-day business.

As individuals mature, their need and capacity to be self-directed, to use their experience in learning, to identify their own readiness to learn, and to organize learning around 'real life' challenges and problems increases rapidly. This concept can also be applied to individual progression through developmental periods in the CF. Andragogical methodologies of education and professional development encourage the concept of self-development and start with the premise that adults need to know why they need to learn something before undertaking to learn it. This is where tools like the 360° evaluation/performance appraisals, exposure to role models through mentoring or coaching, and diagnostic performance assessment play an important role in raising the level of awareness of the need to know.[5] Andragogical methodologies encourage the learner to take increasing responsibility for their own learning which will increase the effectiveness of CF members across learning experiences, deployments and assignments throughout their careers. A new professional development model using more active methods of delivery is based on precepts that mirror other competencies of CF leaders:

> ... adults need to know why they need to learn something; adults maintain the concept of responsibility for their own decisions, their own lives; adults enter the education activity with a greater volume and more varied experiences than do children; adults have a readiness to learn those things that they need to know in order to cope effectively with real-life situations; adults are life-centered in their orientation to learning; and adults are more responsive to internal motivators than external motivators.[6]

Analysis conducted by Dr. Leonard Wong and a team of researchers at the Strategic Studies Institute, US Army War College generalized that there are three common developmental tenants – operational assignments, institutional education and self-development.[7] (Mentorship was also included as an influence in the self-developmental process.) When participants were asked to rank these factors as those contributing most to senior leader development, all operational occupations ranked operational assignments (experience) as highest and support occupations ranked either education or headquarters experience as number one. However, one point that was consistent was the requirement for a broad range of experience across a career, starting earlier in the career. The US Army took this research one step further by studying experience more specifically. The researchers concluded that learning from experience is highly beneficial but is affected by the amount of challenge, variety of tasks or assignments, and quality of feedback.[8]

Research conducted with senior DND and CF leaders in 2005 confirmed similar findings to the US studies and further quantified the impact of experience, taking into consideration the timing of certain key postings within a career, location, and posting.

Can andragogy, with its emphasis on incorporating life experiences into the learning process, be an appropriate means to foster learning a new job or skill? Many researchers and scholars answer "Yes." Putman and Bell asserted that, "since older learners will naturally have more life experience, learning specialists will need to find better ways to capitalize on that experience in a learning area."[9]

It is critical that CF senior leaders learn how to think critically, conceptually, and creatively when confronted with situations needing analysis and when developing solutions to problems. They must also have the needed skills and mental capacities to learn from and be able to apply their experiences. Adult learning techniques emphasise experience and situational training that, research has proven, enhance problem solving and critical thinking.

What makes andragogical professional development different from training and education? Theories of adult learning attempt to differentiate the way adults learn. A number of assumptions are made based on Knowles' theory that "adults are autonomous and self-directed; adults are goal oriented; adults are relevancy oriented (problem centered) — they need to know why they are learning something; adults are practical and problem-solvers; and adults have accumulated life experiences."[10] Not only do adults learn differently than children but they are motivated differently. Motivating factors include the ability to connect socially, meeting external expectations (require upgrade to keep job or be promoted); better customer service; advancement; escape or stimulation; and pure interest or enjoyment.[11] Faculty should be aware of the possible motivators and take this into consideration when designing courses and instructional materials for adult professional development.

Despite the positive evidence in favour of andragogical approaches to education and professional development, the theory of andragogy is not without its critics and there have been arguments made against aspects of andragogy and self-directed learning. These tend to focus on the nature of subject matter and situation rather than the actual application of the techniques proposed.

The effectiveness of professional development depends to a great extent on how well programs are designed. The design should take into account learning theory, the specific learning objectives, characteristics of the participants, and practical considerations such as constraints and costs in relation to benefits. Yukl makes the point that "leadership training is more likely to be successful if designed and conducted in a way that is consistent with some important finds in research on learning processes and training techniques."[12] These include clear-learning objectives; clear, meaningful content; appropriate sequencing of content; an appropriate mix of methods; opportunity for application and active practice; relevant, timely feedback; enhancement of self-confidence and appropriate follow-up activities.[13]

CF research participants were asked to list and rate the conditions that would enhance the success of professional development. Their responses were consistent with the research and included (in order of importance) time, method, systems approach (integrated and interrelated), value for individual, accessibility, learning climate, chain of command support, and value for the organization.

Studies continue to confirm the complex nature of the 21st century workplace and the need to better support workers as they grow, enhancing their skills and competencies to meet the demands of the changing nature of work. Review of a range of executive development programs currently offered clearly indicates that serveral characteristics are common to the most successful civilian and miltary professional development programs. These features include (1) a competency framework, (2) program individualization for participants, and (3) mechanisms to ensure that learning and its transfer into the workplace are supported and embraced by the sponsoring organization. Almost all successful executive development programs have a leadership competency model, management support, systematic training, flexibility, and action learning that involves interactive learning, coaching, mentoring and feedback.

Although the the most recent CF research examined the current professional development options and challenges faced by current senior leaders in a variety of positions and organizations within the CF, there is every indication that future senior CF leaders will be faced with similar challenges and ever increasing demands. Research confirmed that there is a requirement to better prepare senior leaders earlier in their careers through experience, assessment and evaluation that provides meaningful feedback, and flexible professional development utilizing a wider range of options that begin at the rank of Major (when first assigned with greater leadership responsibility) and extend across a career.

How do we enhance the current system of professional development to better prepare CF senior leaders, given the diverse and complex nature of their corporate and governance responsibilities with DND and the stewardship of the profession of arms and military leadership with the CF? The answers provided by participants of the 2005 research study were varied but consistent with the literature on adult learning, professional development and strategic leader development.

Several common themes were identified by emerging and senior CF leaders in the search for more effective professional and leader development. These include leader capacities and competencies, education, experience and employment, evaluation tools and performance appraisals, mentoring and coaching, governance and how government works, and life-long learning. Literature and data collected from CF members confirmed that much of the skill essential for effective leadership is gained through experience rather than formal training.

Members interviewed rated experience on par with education as a critical factor influencing the effectiveness of senior leaders. Experience was not limited to inside the CF and external experience was seen a providing a better understanding of departmental organizations and appointments. What was deemed most critical to CF strategic leaders was time to think and observe, direct staff experience in strategic planning or policy, and informal mentoring arrangements. Two key factors influencing success in certain positions and in similar situations in the future were the opportunity to understudy to a key position and with a capable person. Superiors can provide valuable coaching and mentoring to help members learn new skills and to interpret their job, but there is equally valuable experience in learning what not to do from supervisors who are ineffective.

Experts in the field and CF members interviewed agreed that success in handling difficult challenges is essential for leadership development and prepares leaders with greater self-confidence and skill. Learning from experience means facing failures as well as successes. A research study conducted by Gary Yukl for the Centre for Creative Leadership concluded that those who experienced failure and adversity earlier in their careers were more likely to develop and advance to a higher level than those who experience only a series of early successes.[14]

CF members also commented upon the fact that experience should build upon past challenges and start with very tactical military expertise dealing with the situation, mission, command and control, etc. They felt that the CF spent far more time going into depth at this level because this is what CF members needed to do in operations. The challenge for the CF is to use this as the foundation on which to build senior, institutional leadership, and what was needed was a better set of building blocks at the higher levels. Another related observation by one participant was that members spend a great deal of work time in a three-year posting learning how to do the job. Little time is actually spent doing the job or tackling the issues within that job. This begs the questions – how effective can we be in those jobs and how effective is that experience?

The general consensus in the CF is that the wider the experience of CF members, the better able they are to adapt. One senior leader noted that the CF cannot take a junior officer and simply 'educate' or 'train' them to be a senior leader, as experience was critical. This included the notion that senior leaders should have had a series of postings to headquarters including National Defence Headquarters (NDHQ) long before they are assigned a position of strategic leadership. There is a challenge deciding when and where to put people who show potential – too early and they may not be able to rise to the challenge, too late and you've missed the opportunity for development. There are some skills you cannot acquire without experience working at the institutional level at a variety of ranks.

International postings and postings to other government departments and central agencies rated high on the scale for beneficial experience and development for senior CF leaders. Working outside of Canada and the institution provided a greater range and depth of experiences in increasingly more responsible positions for many of the study respondents. One participant observed that the public service have an advantage because they can be developed in a single stream and gain experience in related positions (this concept was further developed by another participant who noted the public service have had only experience and very little professional development until recent years). Military specialist officers can be developed along a career stream to a certain extent. Mapping the career path for support officers involved in this study proved that there was a more linear career track through progressive experiences that included exposure to some of the key organizations and activities that are considered to be challenges for today's senior CF leader. However, at the highest levels of institutional leadership it was felt that there are more jobs 'designated' or 'reserved' for operators but they too need more experience and education outside of the theatre of operations to better prepare them.

Growth and learning are enhanced when experiences are diverse as well as challenging. Diversity requires adaptation and critical thinking that is beneficial to development and performance. Providing a range of opportunities can be a challenge with a force the size of the CF but special assignments, secondments, acting positions, exchanges, and career management can provide wider experience and development.

Experience gained through situational leadership assists in preparing leaders to adapt to changing conditions that are not under their control. It can provide learning experiences when ingenuity is brought to the forefront to compensate for errors or deficiencies. Strong adaptive leadership can result in providing the leader with an opportunity to confirm or discover personal capacities including courage.

Leader capacities can be enhanced through professional development that includes the four pillars of education, training, experience, and self-development. A component of self-development and experience is self-awareness, and this includes providing feedback in a variety of means.

More learning occurs from experience when this is combined with accurate and relevant feedback. This is seldom provided for operational assignments as there may be no direct observation of senior leaders by their superiors and the pace of activity may not allow for debriefs or self-analysis.[15] The same challenge occurs at senior levels when strategic leaders tend to become isolated or grouped in small numbers.

In recent years there has been increasing interest in mentoring and executive coaching. While the CF have been slow to initiate formal programs of this nature, informal mentoring and coaching have occurred with supervisor and subordinate relationships throughout the organization. A Corporate Leadership Council survey conducted in 2003 to look at qualities of CEO's that contributed to success reported that 'having a mentor' rated #3 behind 'personal drive' and 'personal value system' and ahead of 'learning from mistakes' and 'being a team player'.[16]

Despite the many potential benefits from mentoring, it is not always successful and there are specific conditions that are more likely to improve the effectiveness of mentoring. Some research suggests that informal mentoring is more successful then formal mentoring programs. R. Noe found that personality conflicts and lack of mentor commitment were more likely to occur with assigned mentors. The success of mentoring can be increased by using a semi-formal approach that allows for voluntary participation, with some structure and support.[17]

Research indicates that, for a successful mentoring connection, the mentor and the protégé must both support the relationship and be willing to commit time and energy to the process. The essential elements are respect, trust, partnership building, realistic expectations and self-perception, and time.[18]

In general, research suggests that mentoring can be a useful technique for facilitating career advancement, adjustment to change, and job satisfaction of a protégé.[19] Supervisors can serve as mentors to a certain extent but the most effective mentor is not the first or second level supervisor. Mentoring is more successful when the mentor is about two grade levels above the protégé.[20]

While coaching can be considered an element of mentoring, there are differences between the two. Some experts in coaching would distinguish mentoring from coaching as follows: "Mentors empower their protégés to find answers by sharing their knowledge and experience with them. Coaches provide answers by encouraging individuals to use their own life experiences and competencies."[21]

The top ten methodologies suggested by research participants to enhance CF professional development were experience, developmental activities, seminars, case studies, performance measurement, courses, post-graduate education, mentoring or coaching, outsourced professional development and self-directed professional development.

This is not an exhaustive list and represents only the most prevalent responses collected by the researcher in a 2005 CF study. It is worthy of note that the more interactive methods ranked higher on the scale than passive, self-directed methodologies. The majority of participants felt that they would be more likely to participate in and benefit from more 'hands on', practical forms of professional development than simply being informed of resources or opportunities that were accessible through the Internet, virtual library or Intranet. This is also consistent with literature on adult learning and executive professional development that recommends 'action learning' approaches that engage the learner in finding 'real solutions to real problems'.[22]

Experience was a term used to cover a range of activities including practical experience in a job setting, exercise, or simulator; and a job posting for a specified employment period or acting time. Examples in this category were generally meant to be more 'hands on' and practical than the other methods mentioned and this was considered critical to participants. Experience was differentiated from 'expertise' in comments as participants spoke in more general terms of what a senior leader could gain through experience. In addition to professional development, experience was also related to personnel management and postings.

The types of programs suggested were also related to time, accessibility and availability. Participants who were familiar with mentoring and coaching spoke very favourably of those experiences but underscored that this was 'new turf' for the CF and a formal program might detract from the informal mentoring and coaching that is highly successful in the current system.

The most popular options were short duration, local seminars. There was interest in including senior leaders from other Departments for common themes or exchange of information. However, time and commitment required outside of the office factored heavily in the type of program recommended by participants and their willingness to participate in these types of programs.

When discussing an enhanced professional development program with CF members, time was considered to be the greatest impediment and/or concern to current senior military and civilian leaders who struggle to find a balance between work responsibilities and personal life, let alone professional development. The choice of methods and options for future professional development was indicative of the finite amount of time these leaders have. One commented that "unless it is booked into the calendar, it doesn't get done." Location was a factor in considering attendance at professional development activities. There were advantages and disadvantages to local and distance options as local seminars were prime for cancellations or distractions from the office, but off-site increased the amount of time necessary to attend. Consideration of any additions to the CF Professional Development System (CFPDS) must take into account the need for maximum flexibility to achieve the best possible balance.

The vision is a Canadian Forces that is fully professional, aware of its responsibilities to the nation, and which manifests those qualities and ideals inherent in the military ethos upon which military effectiveness depends. It calls for men and women who are outstanding leaders and who demonstrate superior intellectual capacity based on a broad liberal education. They will be dynamic and flexible in thought and action, capable of dealing with uncertainty and ambiguity, innovative and proactive. They will operate effortlessly in a technological and information rich environment and be committed to life-long learning.[23]

While there have been numerous historical studies and recommendations to enhance leadership and professional development, gaps remain between what the current system provides and the perceived need of the organization and its members. Despite identified gaps, it should be noted that there has been extensive improvement to leadership and professional development across the CF. However, the Officer Professional Development Program is in a state of flux at several levels and after implementation of recommendations following an end-to-end review of Officer Professional Development by the Canadian Defence Academy in 2003.[24]

There is no question that developing and implementing an effective professional development system is a complex problem. The time, resources and people required to make the system effective is a challenge in and of itself. The

CFPDS is further complicated by the conflicting priorities and competing demands of key stakeholders with DND and the CF. None of the participants of the 2005 study was happy with the status quo. However, there was near unanimous agreement that the basic CFPDS Framework of four pillars – Education, Experience, Training and Self-Development, and the four Developmental Periods were sound and, for the foreseeable future, the critical factors impacting professional development would continue to be time and money.

In this study and in the CDA End to End Review of Officer Professional Development conducted in 2003, there was a broad spectrum of views regarding the need for CFPDS and Officer Professional Development reform. A small minority regarded the thrust for OPD reform as "unnecessary and an over-reaction to excessively publicized scandals of the 1990s", more recent government scandals involving leadership and the current CDS transformation agenda. A much larger group felt that OPD reform was essential for the continued health of the CF and effective leadership of the institution. Notwithstanding this, for those in favour of enhancing professional development, there were varied opinions as to what that would constitute the addressing of the balance between the education and experience pillars.

Experience rated highest amongst factors influencing success of senior institutional leaders, and we must review and adapt not only our employment model but evaluation and selection methods to ensure that members of the CF are well prepared in all respects for the responsibilities of institutional leadership. 'Development' and 'employment' were seen to be in conflict in our current system as we are "too busy working to train" with the present pace of operations, transformation and day-to-day business. As stated earlier, this could be eased though the introduction of a wider range of methodologies of professional development that include mentoring and coaching, multi-rater feedback, seminars, e-learning and part-time education.

When the CF effectiveness outcomes are mapped against the five CF leader elements – expertise, cognitive capacities, social capacities, change capacities and professional ideology –and then applied to the current model of professional development across the four pillars of experience, training, education and self-development, thereby creating the CF Professional Development Framework (see Chapter 7 and Figure 6, repeated here), further gaps in the current system can be identified and a new, more effective system can be designed to provide CF leaders with a range of options to develop not only the leader elements but the capacities.[25]

	Expertise	Cognitive Capacities	Social Capacities	Change Capacities	Professional Ideology
Senior	Strategic	Creative Abstract	Inter-Institutional	Paradigm Shifting	Stewardship
Advanced	↑	↑	↑	↑	↑
Intermediate					
Junior	Tactical	Analytical	Inter-Personal	Open	Internalize

THE PROFESSIONAL DEVELOPMENT FRAMEWORK

Utilizing the five leader elements of the framework, it is possible to project the foundation of an enhanced CFPDS and progressive system from junior leaders to senior leaders as illustrated in the figure above. The development of the elements is presented in a progressive manner to emphasize that there is sequencing in development of capacities from junior through intermediate to advanced and senior leader positions. The more senior levels are founded on the development of strategic capabilities as illustrated at the highest level of the framework.

"WHERE THE RUBBER HITS THE ROAD"

The foregoing text constituted an integration of the generic research and perspectives on pedagogical and andragogical learning strategies with the general circumstances of current professional development in the CF. The subsequent text, below, is aimed at synthesizing this collated information above in order to apply it, with some emphasis, to a reformation proposal for CF professional development for senior leaders over the near future years. This paper ends, appropriately, with conclusions.

Unfortunately, a shift from the status quo requires a dramatic change in perspective that does not come naturally to an organization as large and complex as the CF, but the increased demands facing senior leaders will require a transition from our pedagogical approach geared towards training and operations to an adult-oriented model that includes methods emphasizing discovery of knowledge and confirmation through experience and professional development. This requires a change of perspective for instructors as well as students as the classic role of the teacher being the only subject matter expert with complete control and responsibility for the learning changes dramatically with the application of contemporary adult learning methodologies. This method does "everything possible to provide the learner with whatever foundational content needed and then encourages a self-directed process of further inquiry."[26] As emphasized above, Malcolm Knowles' theory of andragogy relies on the fact that adults are capable of self-directed learning and this method allows the learner to move to independent learning as quickly as possible.

Research has provided an ever increasing source of detailed information that has increased our understanding of how to facilitate adult learning. Learning theory has advanced so that we have "expanded thinking/cognitive/learning style models to organize vast amounts of information."[27] Senior leaders have an increased demand for enhanced critical thinking skills and a better understanding of how to manipulate the learning environment to attain competencies such as this. Executive leadership development and professional development within organizations has been on the rise and there are increased demands for effective and efficient programs. This is the case with the CF.

The challenges of making the transition to senior leadership typically fall into five broad categories:

a. Influencing others more effectively, particularly upwardly and outwardly;

b. Thinking strategically;

c. Achieving a better balance in handling short-term and long-term pressures;

d. Moving from a functional or departmental perspective to a broader organizational perspective; and

e. Actually creating or influencing organizational strategy.[28]

Easing the transition of military senior leaders to strategic leadership means proactivity in preparing potential leaders at earlier stages of their careers, beginning with the rank of Major at DP 3 so that they are better prepared for future responsibilities. This is still a team effort across the CF as "strategic leadership is now the responsibility of many people, not just those at the top."[29]

"Strategic leadership is about becoming. It's a process of never-ending individual, team and organizational learning."[30] In the simplest of terms, we can use Dr. Leonard Wong's (American) reference, above, that "a strategic leader must 'Be, Know, and Do' just about everything."[31] To achieve that goal, the CF will require a more flexible and comprehensive professional development system that caters to the needs and learning styles of adults, based on a competency based framework and includes an employment model that allows for vicarious learning through a range of ever more challenging experiences, broad education at the undergraduate and graduate level, experiences outside of the institution, mentoring and/or coaching, more comprehensive and effective feedback and performance assessment tools and access to options and material for continuous self-development. The system must balance education and experience while contributing to retention and morale of the CF. The CFPDS must provide sufficient choice, flexibility and accessibility to encourage and facilitate professional development while making the CF a career of choice.

There are eight strategic objectives to be fulfilled by the professional development system in order to achieve the vision communicated in *Officership 2020*. Importantly, several apply directly to the professional development system, including the application of sound leadership; the highest standard of professionalism; officers who think critically; officers who embrace and manage change; transforming the CF into a learning organization; establishing the policies and conditions that create a 'career of choice' environment; and governance that allows for flexibility of the ODP system. Key actions to achieve these strategic objectives also apply to professional development – ensure intellectual development; improve the common body of knowledge; develop policy, concepts and doctrine; strengthen the military ethos; cultivate external relationships and links; provide OPD flexibility; provide organizational capacity and resourcing; and establish accountabilities, incentives and performance measurement.[32]

Keeping pace with rapid change is one of the greatest challenges facing leaders today. Dealing with the immediate demands and crises often leaves little time to consider and prepare for the challenges of tomorrow. Formal courses would be outdated before they were taught. Professional development must respond to changing demands and issues.

Advances in military technology well represent rapid change, especially in key capability areas such as command, control, communications, computers, intelligence, surveillance and reconnaissance. Such technologies have improved the effectiveness of military forces while at the same time imposing challenges in terms of maintaining interoperability among allied and like-minded forces. While technology may be considered as part of the 'training' pillar of the CFPDS, changes and enhancements to technology will impact across the entire system and senior leaders must be familiar with what is available and how to utilize it. Professional development programs will have to include greater use of technology to a greater extent to achieve efficiencies for delivery.

DND and the CF continue to adjust to the changing age, ethnic makeup and job expectations of the Canadian population and work force. Challenges are particularly acute in certain occupational areas where the Canadian Forces must compete with private sector employers for highly qualified personnel. Senior leaders must be prepared to address diversity and changing demographics.

SUMMARY AND CONCLUSIONS

In 2005, the Chief of Defence Staff initiated a CF-wide transformation plan to transform the CF to be more relevant, responsive and effective. Operational effectiveness is central to this transformation but so is institutional alignment, and senior CF leaders will need to be better prepared to take the CF into the future. If professional development fails to keep pace with the demands of the institution, leaders will be left behind.

According to a U.S. Navy Post Graduate School study titled *The Military Officer of 2030*, it was determined "that outside of a short list of universal beneficial leadership traits (e.g. responsible leaders of good character), the specifics of the kind of leader we will need in 30 years is not known."[33] However, the challenges are likely to remain the same. The emphasis on leader professional development must be two-fold: the acquisition of a breadth of knowledge and experience by future leaders in a wide range of CF competencies; and provision of a wealth of potentially qualified members ready to enter institutional leadership positions.

The existing professional development program falls short of these requirements in that it:

    a.   provides little or no support for strategic leaders beyond the rank of Colonel/Captain (N);

b. is founded solely on completion of a limited number of formal courses, one of which has a very limited class size (NSSP) and the other that is not mandatory upon promotion (Brigadier General/Commodore Symposium);

c. does not include a formal support mechanism for strategic leaders to pursue professional development outside the CF;

d. has no formal link to other HR processes that influence a strategic leader's career;

e. has no mentoring or coaching support to guide individuals during completion of learning experiences or new assignments;

f. caters to the collective group (through formal courses), but does not support the individualized learning that may be essential in the performance of a strategic leader's duties; and

g. does not recognize and support informal learning opportunities in the workplace such as knowledge transfer, partnering and networking.[34]

The CF has traditionally utilized 'conventional' methods of education and professional development with the introduction of syndicate and case study work introduced after initial DP training. The Officer Professional Development (OPD) system of today uses both pedagogical and experiential components, an approach proven in practice. "The pedagogical component includes education (knowledge, thinking, reasoning), training (rules, techniques, methods), and socialization (identity, ethics, ethos)."[35] The experiential component includes aspects of formal education and training (university, staff college and classification courses), self-development, and employment.

In developing leaders and facilitating the shift from predominantly leading people to leading the institution, we will require more innovative and interactive methodologies for professional development and adult education. Add to this the concept of life-long learning and it is clear that the CF must recognize the value and importance of continuing the learning process indefinitely outside of the traditional classroom setting. An enhanced professional development program for senior CF leaders must go beyond simply describing a list of concepts and principles. What will be more effective in enhancing the development of senior CF leaders will be an integrative and coherent framework of adult learning for which the label andragogy has been coined to differentiate it from the theory of youth learning or pedagogy.

The world has undergone a number of significant alterations since the end of the Cold War and these changes have, in turn, affected the role requirements and practice of leadership in the CF. New leader responsibilities, requiring new or enhanced competencies have arisen as a result of globalization, changes in the security environment, a changing human resource environment, and a changing public environment. The continuing revolutions in the areas of global conflict, societal values, resource management, and especially in information and technology, all demand that the senior officer of tomorrow possess the knowledge and skills to be an integral component of a new multi-disciplined knowledge-based generation of leaders. It seems obvious that rigorous intellectual development is becoming the overriding, if not the governing factor in the operational and corporate success and effectiveness of the future Canadian Officer Corps.

Participants of the 2005 CF study on professional development all agreed that leadership of the CF is being influenced by a bow wave of change brought about by internal and external influences, not the least of which is the yet to be confirmed internal impact of CF transformation. Externally, demographics are rapidly changing within and around the CF and leaders need to understand and adapt their styles to an array of cultures, generations and lifestyles. Dual income families, service couples, aging parents and an aging work force will also directly impact CF leaders now and into the future, particularly with respect to the value systems of new entry members. Leadership training and professional development will need to include these issues to improve understanding.

The CF requires a professional development program that encourages and supports continual learning and leader development. Many of the attributes that are considered essential to effective leader performance are achievable through an effective professional development program that will enhance our leadership at all levels. Developing and implementing a range of flexible, action-based professional development opportunities, and encouraging the pursuit of personal programs of self-improvement, will ensure that officers and NCMs performing leadership roles will be ready, confident, and able to lead now and into the future.

SELECT BIBLIOGRAPHY

Hughes, R.L., & Beatty, K.C. *Becoming a Strategic Leader.* San Francisco, CA: Jossey-Bass and Center for Creative Leadership, 2005.

Hughes, R., Ginnett, R. and Curphy, G. *Leadership: Enhancing the Lessons of Experience.* Boston, MA: Richard D. Irwin, Inc., 1993.

Knowles, M. S., & Associates. *Andragogy in Action: Applying Modern Principles of Adult Learning.* San Francisco: Jossey-Bass Publishers 1984.

Magee, R. and Burke, B. *Strategic Leadership Primer.* Carlisle Barracks, Pennsylvania: Department of Command, Leadership, and Management U.S. Army War College, 1998.

O'Toole, J. *Leading Change.* San Fransico: Jossey Bass, 1996.

Peters, T. *Re-imagine! Business Excellence in a Disruptive Age.* London: Dorling Kindersley Limited, 2003.

Useem, M. *Leading Up.* New York: Crown Business, Random House Inc., 2001.

Wong, L., Gerras, S., Kidd, W., Pricone, R., Swengros, R. *Strategic Leadership Competencies*. Strategic Studies Institute, US Army War College, 2003.

Yukl, G. *Leadership in Organizations*, Fifth Edition. Upper Saddle River, NJ: A Person Education Company, 2002

Zaccaro, S. *The Nature of Executive Leadership: A Conceptual and Empirical Analysis of Success*. Washington, DC: American Psychological Association, 2001.

ENDNOTES

1   Alan Okros, *Applying the CFLI Leader Framework*, (Canada: Department of Military Psychology and Leadership, Royal Military College, 2004).

2   Canada, *Development Strategy, Model and Implementation Framework for the Professional Development of Strategic Leaders* (Special Advisor to the CDS on Professional Development, 2002).

3   Malcolm Knowles as cited in R. Hiemstra *Lifelong Learning: An Exploration of Adult and Continuing Education Within a Setting of Lifelong Learning Needs,* 3rd Edition. (Fayetteville, New York: 2002).

4   Ibid., 234.

5   Malcolm Knowles, E.F. Holton III, E.F., & R.A. Swanson, R.A., "A theory of adult learning: Andragogy" in *The Adult Learner: The Definitive Classic in Adult Education and Human Resource Development* (5th Edition) (Woburn: Butterworth-Heinemann, 1998). 62.

6   Ibid,. 72.

7   Wong, L., Gerras, S., Kidd, W., Pricone, R., Swengros, R. *Strategic Leadership Competencies*. Strategic Studies Institute, US Army War College, 2003.

8   Mumford, M., Marks, M., Connelly, M., Zaccaro, S. and Reiter-Palmon, R. "Development of Leadership Skills – Experience and Timing" in *Leadership Quarterly*, 11(1), 87-114, 2000.

9   As cited in M.L. Birzer, "The theory of andragogy applied to police training" in *Policing: An International Journal of Police Strategies & Management,* Volume 26 Number 1. (2003), 29-42.

10   J. Blackmore. *Pedagogy: Learning Styles: Preferences* (1996). Retrieved June 16, 2005 from http://www.cyg.net/~jblackmo/diglib/styl-d.html , (1996). 3.

11   Ibid.

12 Gary Yukl, *Leadership in Organizations*: *Custom Edition for LT 516, Royal Roads University.* (Upper Saddle River, New Jersey: Prentice-Hall, 2002).

13 Ibid., 186.

14 Gary Yukl, G.A., *Leadership in Organizations* (5th edition). (Upper Saddle, NJ: Prentice Hall, 2001).

15 Gary Yukl, *Leadership in Organizations: Custom Edition for LT 516, Royal Roads University.* (Upper Saddle River, New Jersey: Prentice-Hall., 2002).

16 RAAF, n.d.

17 Gary Yukl, *Leadership in Organizations: Custom Edition for LT 516*, Royal Roads University. (Upper Saddle River, New Jersey: Prentice-Hall., 2002). 202.

18 USCG, 2000.

19 Gary Yukl, *Leadership in Organizations: Custom Edition for LT 516, Royal Roads University.* (Upper Saddle River, New Jersey: Prentice-Hall., 2002). 203.

20 United State Coast Guard (USCG). *Mentoring Program.* Retrieved June 15, 2005 from http://www.uscg.mil/leadership/mentoring.htm (2002).

21 Naval Reserve. (2003). *Naval Reserve Command Development Mentoring Initiative* (NRCDMI). (Quebec City, QC: Naval Reserve Headquarters, 2003).

22 Giber, D., Carter, L. and Goldsmith, M. (2000) *Best Practices in Leadership Development Handbook.* (San Francisco CA: Linkage Inc, Jossey-Bass/Pfeiffer, 2000) xvi.

23 Romeo Dallaire as cited in *Canada, Canadian Officership in the 21st Century* (*Officership 2020*). Ottawa, ON: DND/CF 2001) 2.

24 Canadian Defence Academy (CDA). The End to End Review of Officer Professional Development. A report produced by the Director of Professional Development, Officer Professional Development staff, 17 November 2003.

25 Robert W. Walker, "The Strategic Operating Concept and the CF Leader Framework", Canadian Forces Leadership Institute, March 1, 2005.

26 Malcolm Knowles, "Andragogy revisited part II." *In Adult Education*, 30, (1979), 52.

27 R. Hiemstra *Lifelong Learning: An Exploration of Adult and Continuing Education Within a Setting of Lifelong Learning Needs,* 3rd Edition. (Fayetteville, New York: 2002) 4.

28 Hughes, R.L., & Beatty, K.C., *Becoming a Strategic Leader.* (San

Francisco, CA: Jossey-Bass and CCL, 2005). ix.

29   Ibid., xii.

30   Ibid., xiii.

31   Wong, L., Gerras, S., Kidd, W., Pricone, R., Swengros, R. *Strategic Leadership Competencies*. (Strategic Studies Institute, US Army War College, 2003). v.

32   Canada, *Canadian Officership in the 21st Century (Officership 2020)*. (Ottawa, ON:DND/CF, 2001).

33   W.F. Ulmer, W.F., 'Military Leadership into the 21st Century: Another "Bridge Too Far?"'. *Parameters*, Spring 1998, 54.

34   Canada, *Special Advisor to the CDS on Professional Development (SA PD). Development Strategy, Model and Implementation Framework for the Professional Development of Strategic Leaders*. (Ottawa: CF, 2002).

35   Vice-Chief of Defence Staff. (March 8, 2001). *Strategic Guidance for the CF Officer Corps and the OPD System*. Ottawa, ON: DND.

CONCLUSION

Without question, the obligations placed on those who lead the institution are great. That responsibility demands a whole new set of capabilities, knowledge and orientations for leaders who seek and accept the privilege of contributing to the defence of Canada and serving the people of the world, particularly in light of the complex security environment in which we find ourselves. Becoming a senior leader is daunting, however, being an institutional leader presents the greatest challenge. Institutional leaders manage a constant state of risk. They make tough ethical and moral decisions, often without the luxury of time or complete transparency of mitigating factors. Institutional leaders act in the best interests of the CF and Canadians. They possess and utilize the moral courage to challenge higher authority when there is a need, but also are ready to accept that decisions resulting from due process and consultation regardless of their personal perspectives and intent. They do this on behalf of Canadians and as responsible professionals who are an integral component of the democratic process.

As stated elsewhere in CF leadership publications, the concept of institutional effectiveness – the integration of organizational effectiveness with professional effectiveness – provides the focus for the application of institutional leadership excellence. All leaders in the CF are obligated to continue to hone their expertise, professionalism, and leadership capacities throughout their careers. However, for senior leaders, that honing process includes a continuous focus on leading the institution.

In summary, this book, *Institutional Leadership in the Canadian Forces: Contemporary Issues*, offers practical information covering a range of institutional leader challenges and responsibilities: ascending from the decade of darkness, the 1990's; understanding current issues of CF culture; defining Canadian defence professionals; articulating Canada's way in war; applying requisite ethics as senior leaders; and configuring professional development strategies for institutional

195

leaders in order to guide both those in senior positions and those institutional leaders conscientious about the professional development of their successors. As articulated by the Commander, CDA, Major-General Hussey, in his foreword to this book, the future of the CF is the responsibility of every leader who accepts the challenge of leading the CF institution. Accepting those challenges demands a commitment to career-long professional development. In no other way will CF institutional leaders be prepared for and effective in the future complex responsibilities of the next generation. The publication, dedicated to understanding *Contemporary Issues*, is but foundational information available now to current institutional leaders committed to that future.

CONTRIBUTORS

Captain (Navy) Jennifer J. Bennett served on the staff of the Canadian Defence Academy from 2003 to 2005 as the Ottawa Detachment Commander and Director Professional Development. She is a Naval Reserve officer with two command appointments in Maritime Command and Director level appointments at National Defence Headquarters including Director of Reserves and Director of Training and Education Policy. Captain (Navy) Bennett holds a Bachelor of Physical Education, Bachelor of Education, and Master of Arts in Leadership and Training. Research conducted during her Masters program at Royal Roads University was the basis for the chapter on professional development in this book. In civilian life, Captain (Navy) Bennett is an educator who has taught at the elementary and secondary levels in Ontario and British Columbia. She currently is the Head of School at Fern Hill School in Oakville.

Dr. L. William Bentley, MSM, CD graduated from the Royal Military College in 1970 and served in the infantry in the Royal Canadian Regiment for 35 years. Lieutenant-Colonel Bentley served as the Assistant Defence Advisor to the Canadian Ambassador to NATO and subsequently, on secondment to the Department of Foreign Affairs in Ottawa, as the Director of Peacekeeping. In 1999, he joined Lieutenant-General Romeo Dallaire in the Office of the Special Advisor to the Chief of the Defence Staff for Professional Development. He was the Team Leader for the development and production of *Officership 2020*, the *Non-Commissioned Officer Corps 2020* and *Duty With Honour: The Profession of Arms in Canada*. In 2002, he joined CFLI as the Section Head for Professional Concepts. His book, *Professional Ideology and the Profession of Arms*, was published in 2005. Dr. Bentley has a Master's Degree in International Relations and a Master's Degree in Military Arts and Science, as well as a PhD from the University of Western Ontario. He received the Chief of the Defence/Deputy Minister Innovation Award in 2004 for his work on the Canadian profession of arms manual. He was awarded the Meritorious Service Medal in 2005 for his contributions to professional development in the CF.

Lieutenant-Commander (retired) Karen D. Davis is the senior Defence Scientist at the Canadian Forces Leadership Institute, holds a Master of Arts in Sociology from McGill University and is a PhD candidate at the Royal Military College of Canada. She joined the CF in 1978 as an oceanographic operator, was commissioned in 1989 as a Personnel Selection officer, and 'retired' in 2000. She has conducted research in the Canadian Forces for over 15 years on a range of human resource related issues including gender integration and strategic human resources. With CFLI since 2004, Karen is currently editing a volume on women and leadership, conducting research on measures of leadership and cultural intelligence in the CF, and is a contributing writer to *Leadership in the Canadian Forces: Leading the Institution*.

Colonel Bernd Horn is the Director of the Canadian Forces Leadership Institute. He is an experienced infantry officer with command appointments at the unit and sub-unit level. He was the Commanding Officer of 1 Royal Canadian Regiment (RCR) (2001-2003); the Officer Commanding 3 Commando, the Canadian Airborne Regiment (1993-1995); and the Officer Commanding "B" Company, 1 RCR (1992-1993). Colonel Horn holds an MA and PhD in War Studies from the Royal Military College of Canada / RMC and is an Adjunct-Associate Professor of History at RMC.

Dr. Daniel Lagacé-Roy is a researcher in Military Ethics and Leadership at the Canadian Forces Leadership Institute and an Assistant Professor at the Canadian Defence Academy. He is teaching *Military Professionalism and Ethics* at the Royal Military College of Canada. His research projects are: *Ethics in the Canadian Forces: Tough Choices* (workbook and instructor manual), *Military Ethical Dilemmas, Ethics and Leadership, Introduction to Ethics, Ethical Reasoning and Moral Development*. He previously taught Ethics at the Dufferin-Peel Catholic School Board in Mississauga (ON), at the Université du Québec in Rimouski (QC) and at the University of Alberta in Edmonton (AB). He served in the Canadian Forces from 1987 to 1995 (Regular) and from 1998 to 2001 (Reserves). Dr. Lagacé-Roy received his PhD (Philosophie) from the Université de Montréal (QC).

Brian McKee is a Defence Scientist with Director Personnel Applied Research within Chief of Military Personnel. Prior to working in the Department of National Defence, he occupied a number of senior positions in private sector Human Resource and survey research companies. He has a Masters degree in Sociology from Carleton University and Bachelors degrees in Social Studies and Social Anthropology from Queen's University of Belfast.

Dr. Robert W. Walker, CD, a graduate of the Royal Military College of Canada and Queen's University, served for 21 years in the Royal Canadian Navy and the Canadian Forces as an officer cadet, a naval officer and a personnel selection specialist. He next served with the Royal Canadian Mounted Police (RCMP) for 17 years as a psychologist and civilian member of the Force. During his RCMP career, he oversaw the research and program development department of the Canadian Police College in Ottawa and, subsequently, the development of RCMP commissioning officer qualifying processes and senior executive qualifying processes. Dr. Walker joined CFLI in 2002 in an Associate Professor position. He is engaged in research and publishing on leadership, leader capacities and attributes, and professional development strategies.